Certificate Paper C02

2011 Syllabus

FUNDAMENTALS OF FINANCIAL ACCOUNTING

For assessments in 2015

CIMA

Study Text

In this 2015 edition

- A **user-friendly format** for easy navigation

- Regular **fast forward** summaries emphasising the key points in each chapter

- **Assessment focus points** showing you what the assessor will want you to do

- **Questions** and **quick quizzes** to test your understanding

- **Question bank** containing objective test questions with answers

- A full index

BPP Learning Media's **i-Pass** product also supports this paper.

FOR ASSESSMENTS IN 2015

BPP LEARNING MEDIA

First edition July 2011
Second edition October 2012

ISBN 9781 4453 6471 1
Previous ISBN 9781 4453 7777 3
eISBN 9781 4453 9118 0

British Library Cataloguing-in-Publication Data
A catalogue record for this book is available from the
British Library

Published by

BPP Learning Media Ltd
BPP House, Aldine Place
142-144 Uxbridge Road
London W12 8AA

www.bpp.com/learningmedia

Printed in the United Kingdom by Polestar Wheatons

Hennock Road
Marsh Barton
Exeter
EX2 8RP

Contents

The BPP Learning Media Study Text

Aims of this Study Text

To provide you with the knowledge and understanding, skills and application techniques that you need if you are to be successful in your exams

This Study Text has been written to cover the 2011 **Fundamentals of Financial Accounting** syllabus.

- It is **comprehensive**. It covers the syllabus content. No more, no less.
- It is written at the **right level**. Each chapter is written with CIMA's precise learning outcomes in mind.
- It is targeted to the **assessment**. We have taken account of guidance CIMA has given and the assessment methodology.

To allow you to study in the way that best suits your learning style and the time you have available, by following your personal Study Plan (see page (vii))

You may be studying at home on your own until the date of the exam, or you may be attending a full-time course. You may like to (and have time to) read every word, or you may prefer to (or only have time to) skim-read and devote the remainder of your time to question practice. Wherever you fall in the spectrum, you will find the BPP Learning Media Study Text meets your needs in designing and following your personal Study Plan.

To tie in with the other components of the BPP Learning Media Effective Study Package to ensure you have the best possible chance of passing the exam (see page (v))

Learning to Learn Accountancy

BPP Learning Media's ground-breaking **Learning to Learn Accountancy** book is designed to be used both at the outset of your CIMA studies and throughout the process of learning accountancy. It challenges you to consider how you study and gives you helpful hints about how to approach the various types of paper which you will encounter. It can help you **focus your studies on the subject and exam**, enabling you to **acquire knowledge**, **practise and revise efficiently and effectively**.

The BPP Learning Media Effective Study Package

Recommended period of use	The BPP Learning Media Effective Study Package
From the outset and throughout	**Learning to Learn Accountancy** Read this invaluable book as you begin your studies and refer to it as you work through the various elements of the BPP Learning Media Effective Study Package. It will help you to acquire knowledge, practise and revise, efficiently and effectively.
Three to twelve months before the assessment	**Study Text and Interactive Passcards** Use the Study Text and Interactive Passcards to acquire knowledge, understanding, skills and the ability to apply techniques.
Throughout	**i-Pass** **i-Pass**, our computer based testing package, provides objective test questions in a variety of formats and is ideal for self-assessment.
One to six months before the assessment	**Practice & Revision Kit** Try the numerous assessment-format questions, for which there are full worked solutions where relevant prepared by BPP Learning Media's own authors. Then attempt the two mock assessments.
From three months before the assessment until the last minute	**Passcards** Work through these short, memorable notes which are focused on what is most likely to come up in the assessment you will be sitting.

BPP LEARNING MEDIA

Introduction   v

1 What is accounting?

Accounting is the process of collecting, recording, summarising and communicating financial information.

Question
Accounting

(a) You will often meet with the terms 'an accounting statement' or 'a set of accounts'. Do you know what is meant by these terms?

(b) Who do you think has the task of preparing accounting statements? In an organisation of a reasonable size, would it be one person? One department? Several different departments?

(c) Who are the users of accounting information?

(d) What is the purpose of accounting?

Answer

(a) An accounting statement is, for example, an income statement or a statement of financial position. A set of accounts is a number of accounting statements presented together with the intention of showing an overall view of an organisation's income, expenditure, assets and liabilities.

(b) Most organisations of reasonable size will have at least one accounts department, staffed by people with detailed knowledge of accounting systems and theory. In large organisations there may be several departments, or groups, responsible for preparing accounting information to meet the different needs of accounts users.

(c) The users of accounts include a variety of people and organisations, both internal and external, as explained in Section 2 of this chapter, such as current and potential workers, investors, customers and suppliers. Government bodies and the general public may also be interested. The extent of their information needs varies widely.

(d) There are many purposes of accounting. You may have considered the following.

- Control over the use of resources
- Knowledge of what the business owes and owns
- Calculation of profits and losses
- Cash budgeting
- Effective financial planning

1.1 Why keep accounts?

Accounting information is essential to the efficient running of a business. It helps managers to control the use of resources, keep track of the assets and liabilities of the business and plan effectively for the future.

Accounts show where money came from and how it has been spent, this

- **aids** the efficient running of a business
- **indicates** how successfully managers are performing
- **provides information** about the resources and activities of a business

4.3 Accruals concept

The **accruals concept** means that incomo a
are earned or incurred, not received or paid

Assessment focus point — The accruals concept is very important as it

It is very important to grasp that, in nearly a
basis. This is because cash accounting doe

4.4 Example: accruals concep

Emma has a business printing and selling T

Invoice date	Numbers boug
Purchases	
7.5.X7	20
Sales	
8.5.X7	4
12.5.X7	6
23.5.X7	10

What is Emma's profit for May?

Solution

Cash basis
    Sales
    Purchases
    Profit/loss
Accruals basis
    Sales ($40 + $60 + $100)
    Purchases
    Profit

The accruals basis gives a truer picture than
her customers are legally bound to pay her a

Her statement of financial position as at 31 M

Assets
    Receivables ($40 + $60 + $100)

Proprietor's capital
Liabilities
Payables

Accounting information **aids** the efficient running of a business in many ways.

(a) A business needs to pay bills for the goods and services it purchases, and collect money from its customers. It must, therefore, keep a record of such bills and invoices so that the correct amounts can be paid or collected at the correct times.

(b) Keeping records of a business's assets (eg its motor vehicles or computers) helps to keep them secure

Accounts **indicate how successfully** the managers are performing.

Modern businesses are often complicated, they seldom have a single owner (some very large enterprises, such as J Sainsbury, may be owned by millions of shareholders). Frequently the owners are not involved in the day-to-day running of the business but appoint managers to act on their behalf. In addition, there are too many activities and assets for the managers to keep track of simply from personal knowledge and an occasional glance at the bank statement, so accounts which summarise transactions are very useful.

A business should **provide information** about its resources and activities because there are many groups of people who want or need that information. We will look more closely at the classes of people who might need information about a business in Section 2.

Question — Why keep accounts?

Why should a business keep accounts?

A   To discover how well the business is doing
B   To record assets and liabilities
C   To help run the business efficiently
D   All of the above

Answer

D   All of the above statements are true.

2 Users of accounting information

Accounting information is required for a wide range of users both within and outside the business.

The following people might be interested in financial information about a large public company.

User group	Comment
Managers of the company	People appointed by the company's owners to supervise the daily activities of the company need information about the company's current and expected future financial situation, to make **planning decisions**.
Shareholders of the company, ie the company's owners	Want to assess how effectively management is performing and how much profit they can withdraw from the business for their own use.

Question

Which of the following is a function of [...]

A   Preparing budgets
B   Costing products
C   Setting selling prices
D   Summarising historical accounti[...]

Answer

D   Correct; this is a function of fina[...]
A   This is usually a job for the mana[...]
B   This is usually a job for the mana[...]
C   This is usually a job for the mana[...]

Assessment focus point

Management accounts are for **internal** u[...]
information for decisions affecting the fu[...]
past.

4 The main financial s[...]

FAST FORWARD

The two most important financial statem[...]

4.1 The statement of financ[...]

FAST FORWARD

The **statement of financial position** is a [...]
business at a particular date.

Assets are the business's resources eg b[...]
employees. These are all resources which [...]
money owed to it. These provide the func[...]
the bank or to suppliers: these are liabiliti[...]

4.2 The income statement

FAST FORWARD

The **income statement** is a record of inco[...]

The income statement which forms part c[...]
period of a year, commencing from the da[...]

Management accountants might need qua[...]
the business has more income than exper[...]

Organisations which are not run for profit[...]
account which shows the surplus of inco[...]

4.5 Capital

Key term

Capital is a special form of liability, representing the amount owed by the business to its proprietor(s).

In Emma's case it represents the profit earned in May, which she, as owner of the business, is entitled to in full. Capital will also include the proprietor's initial capital, introduced as cash and perhaps equipment or other assets.

For example, if Emma had begun her business on 30 April 20X7 by opening a business bank account and paying in $100, her statement of financial position immediately after this transaction would look like this.

	$
Assets	
Bank	100
Proprietor's capital	100

On 31 May 20X7 the statement of financial position would look like this.

	$
Assets	
Receivables (customers who owe Emma money)	200
Bank	100
	300
Proprietor's capital	
Brought forward	100
Profit for the period	100
Carried forward	200
Liabilities	
Payables (suppliers to whom Emma owes money)	100
	300

Assessment focus point

This example shows that both the statement of financial position and the income statement are summaries of many transactions.

Question

Capital

By looking at the example of Emma, you may be able to see that there is a simple arithmetical relationship linking capital at the beginning of a period, capital at the end of the period, and profit earned during the period. Can you formulate the relationship?

Answer

The relationship is: opening capital + profit = closing capital. In more complicated examples it would be necessary to make adjustments for new capital introduced during the period, and for any capital withdrawn during the period.

6   8   **1: The nature and objectives of accounting** | Part A Conceptu[...]

10   **1: The nature and objectives of accounting** | Part A Conceptual and regulatory framework

Chapter roundup

- Accounting is the process of collecting, recording, summarising and communicating financial information.

- Accounting information is essential to the efficient running of a business. It helps managers to control the use of resources, keep track of the assets and liabilities of the business and plan effectively for the future.

- Accounting information is required for a wide range of users both within and outside the business.

- Management accounts are produced for internal purposes – they provide information to assist managers in running the business. Financial accounts are produced to satisfy the information requirements of external users.

- The two most important financial statements are the statement of financial position and the income statement.

- The statement of financial position is a list of all the assets owned by a business and all the liabilities owed by a business at a particular date.

- The income statement is a record of income generated and expenditure incurred over a given period.

- The accruals concept means that income and expenses are included in the income statement of the period in which they are earned or incurred, not received or paid.

Quick quiz

1   How has the increasing complexity of modern business contributed to the development of accounting?

    A   Lenders need more information

    B   Government needs more information

    C   Too many transactions, so managers need a means of summarising them

    D   Too many transactions, so investors need a means of summarising them

2   Five categories of people who might use accounting information about a business are:

    (1) _____

    (2) _____

    (3) _____

    (4) _____

    (5) _____

3   Fill in the blanks.

The main distinction between financial accounting and management accounting is that financial accounting provides - _____ information to people _____ the organisation, whereas management accounting provides _____ information to _____ on which they can base _____.

4   Accounting information is limited to items having a monetary value. True or false?

5   Explain briefly:

    (a)   What is a statement of financial position?

    (b)   What is an income statement?

6   Fill in the blanks.

The accruals concept means that _____ and _____ are included in the income statement of the period in which they are _____ or _____ not _____ or _____.

7   Which of the following user groups are **most interested** in the cash position of a business?

A   Investors
B   Government
C   Suppliers
D   Customers

Answers to quick quiz

1   C   There are too many activities for a manager to keep track of by himself and so he needs accounts which summarise transactions to monitor the business' performance.

2   Any five from the following list:

- Managers
- Owners (shareholders)
- Trade contacts
- Providers of finance
- Tax authority
- Employees
- Financial analysts and advisers
- Government and its agencies
- The public

3   The main distinction between financial accounting and management accounting is that financial accounting provides **historical** information to people **outside** the organisation, whereas management accounting provides **forward-looking** information to **management** on which they can base **decisions**.

4   True. Accounting information is limited to items having a monetary value.

5   (a)   A statement of financial position shows all the assets and liabilities of a business at a certain date.
    (b)   An income statement shows the income and expenditure for a period.

6   The accruals concept means that **income** and **expenditure** are included in the income statement of the period in which they are **earned** or **incurred** not **received** or **paid**.

7   C   Suppliers are concerned whether the business has enough cash to pay them what they are owed.

Now try the questions below from the Question Bank

Question numbers
1–4

An introduction to final accounts

Introduction

We have used the terms 'business', 'assets' and 'liabilities' without looking too closely at thoir meaning. It is important to have a thorough understanding of how these terms are used in an accounting context.

Section 3 of the chapter introduces a concept which it is important for you to grasp: the **accounting equation**. You may already realise that a statement of financial position has to balance. You are about to learn why!

A statement of financial position shows the liabilities, capital and assets of a business at a given moment in time. It is like a 'snapshot', since it captures a still image of something which is continually changing. Typically, a statement of financial position is prepared to show the position at the end of the accounting period.

Only the basic details of a statement of financial position are described in this chapter. We will add more detail in later chapters, as we look at other ideas and accounting methods.

The income statement matches the revenue earned in a period with the costs incurred in earning it. It is usual to distingulsh between a gross profit (sales revenue less the cost of goods sold) and a net profit (the gross profit less the expenses of selling, distribution, administration etc).

There is a fair amount to learn before you will be able to prepare these statements yourself. It is important to introduce the financial statements now so you can see the final result. Keep them in mind as you tackle the basics of ledger accounting in the next few chapters.

If you buy an asset which you can use in the business over the next twenty years, it would be misleading to charge all the expenses in the first year. This is the principle behind the important distinction between capital and revenue expenditure which is explored in Section 6 of the chapter.

Topic list	Syllabus references
1 The nature of a business	A (1)
2 The statement of financial position: assets and liabilities	A (1), A (2)
3 The accounting equation	A (1)
4 The statement of financial position	A (1), (2)
5 The income statement	A (1), (2)
6 Capital and revenue expenditure	A (1)

1 The nature of a business

Question

You may already be familiar with certain terms. Can you distinguish, for example, between the terms 'an enterprise', 'a business', 'a company' and 'a firm'?

Answer

An 'enterprise' is the most general term, referring to just about any organisation in which people join together to achieve a common end. In the context of accounting it can refer to a multinational conglomerate, a small club, a local authority and so on *ad infinitum*.

A 'business' is also a very general term, but it does not extend as widely as the term 'enterprise' as it would not include a charity or a local authority. Any organisation existing to trade and make a **profit** could be called a business.

A 'company' is an enterprise constituted in a particular legal form, usually involving limited liability for its members. Companies need not be businesses eg many charities are constituted as companies.

A 'firm' is a much vaguer term. It is sometimes used loosely in the sense of a business or a company. Some writers, more usefully, try to restrict its meaning to that of an unincorporated business (ie a business **not** constituted as a company eg a partnership).

Key term

> A **business** is an organisation which sells something or provides a service with the objective of profit.

Businesses range in size from very small (the local shopkeeper or plumber) to very large (ICI), but the objective of earning profit is common to all of them.

FAST FORWARD

> **Profit** is the excess of income over expenditure. When expenditure exceeds income, the business is running at a **loss**.

One of the jobs of an accountant is to measure income, expenditure and profit. It is not a straightforward exercise and in later chapters we will look at some of the theoretical and practical problems.

1.1 Non-profit-making enterprises

Organisations	Comment
Charities – exist to provide help to the needy.	Must keep expenditure within the level of income or cannot continue in operation.
Public sector organisations – exist to serve the community rather than to make profits.	Include government departments and services (eg the fire service, police force, national health service etc). Can only spend the money allowed to them by the government. Must be cost-conscious.
Certain **clubs and associations** – exist to provide services to their members.	To maintain and improve the services they offer, must ensure that income is at least equal to expenditure.

FAST FORWARD

> All enterprises, profit-making or not, will produce financial statements to provide information to interested parties. For a business, the most important statements are the **statement of financial position** and the **income statement**.

1.2 The business as a separate entity

Financial statements always treat the business as a separate entity.

It is crucial that you understand that the convention adopted in preparing accounts (the *entity concept*) is **always** to treat a business as a separate entity from its owner(s). This applies whether or not the business is recognised in law as a separate entity.

Suppose that Fiona Middleton sets up a business as a hairdresser ('Fiona's Salon'). The law sees no distinction between Fiona Middleton, the individual, and the business known as 'Fiona's Salon'. Any debts of the business which cannot be met from business assets must be met from Fiona's private resources.

However the law recognises a company as a legal entity, quite separate from its owners (the shareholders). A company may acquire assets, incur debts and enter into contracts. If a company's assets become insufficient to meet its liabilities, the company might become 'bankrupt'. The shareholders are not usually required to pay the deficit from their own private resources. The debts belong to the company alone, and the shareholders have limited liability.

Key term

> **Limited liability**: the liability of a shareholder to the company is **limited** to any unpaid amounts for shares issued by the company to the shareholder.

Question
The entity concept

Fill in the missing words to make sure you understand the entity concept and how the law differs from accounting practice.

The entity concept regards a business as a _____ entity, distinct from its_____ . The concept applies to _____ businesses. However, the law only recognises a _____ as a legal entity separate from its _____. The liability of shareholders to the company is _____ to the amount they have not yet paid for their shares.

Answer

The missing words are:

separate; owners; all; company; owners; limited.

2 The statement of financial position: assets and liabilities

The statement of financial position is a list of all the assets owned by a business and all the liabilities owed by it at a particular date.

The income statement is a record of income generated and expenditure incurred over a given period.

2.1 Assets

Key term

> An **asset** is something valuable which a business owns. This in effect represents a right of the business to future economic benefits.

Non-current assets are held and used in operations to generate profit, such as an office building, or a machine. Current assets are held for only a short time with the intention of turning them into cash in the ordinary course of business.

2.2 Examples of assets

Non-current assets	
• Factories	• Plant and machinery
• Office building	• Computer equipment
• Warehouse	• Office furniture
• Delivery vans	
• Lorries	

Current assets	
• Cash	• Money owed by customers
• Raw materials	• Cash and bank accounts
• Finished goods held for sale to customers	

2.3 Liabilities

Key term

A **liability** is something which is owed to somebody else. 'Liabilities' is the accounting term for the amounts a business owes (the debts of the business).

2.4 Examples of liabilities

• A bank loan or bank overdraft
• Amounts owed to suppliers for goods purchased but not yet paid for
• Taxation owed to the government

Assessment focus point

It is essential that you can distinguish between assets and liabilities.

 Question

Questions and liabilities

Classify the following items as non-current assets, current assets or liabilities.

(a) A personal computer used in the accounts department of a retail store
(b) A personal computer on sale in an office equipment shop
(c) Wages due to be paid to staff at the end of the week
(d) A van for sale in a motor dealer's showroom
(e) A delivery van used in a grocer's business
(f) An amount owing to a leasing company for the acquisition of a van

(a)   Non-current asset
(b)   Current asset
(c)   Liability
(d)   Current asset
(e)   Non-current asset
(f)   Liability

2.5 Tangible and intangible assets

Non-current assets can be sub-divided into **tangible** and **intangible** assets

Key terms

> **Tangible assets** (literally assets which can be touched) have a physical presence. Examples include factory buildings, machinery used to make goods for sale and office computers. As you will see, in later chapters, tangible assets are also called **property, plant and equipment**.
>
> **Intangible assets** have no physical presence. Examples include royalties, trademarks and patents. They are also called **intellectual property** because they arise from discoveries or know-how.

2.6 The statement of financial position

As you may remember from the examples in Chapter 1, the statement of financial position is a list of the assets and liabilities (including capital) of the business.

Key term

> **Capital** is the amount owed to the owner of the business by the business.

Owners put in money to start a business, and are owed any profits which are generated by the business.

3 The accounting equation

Formula to learn

> The accounting equation is that in a statement of financial position:
>
> Assets = Capital + Liabilities

FAST FORWARD

> The accounting equation demonstrates that the assets of a business are always equal to the liabilities + capital.

3.1 Example: the accounting equation

On 1 July 20X6, Courtney Spice opened a stall in the market, to sell herbs and spices. She had $2,500 to put into her business.

When the business is set up, it owns the cash that Courtney has put into it, $2,500. But does it owe anything?

The answer is yes. The business is a separate entity in accounting terms. It has obtained its assets (in this example cash) from its owner, Courtney Spice. It therefore owes this amount of money to its owner. If Courtney changed her mind and decided not to go into business after all, the business would have to repay the cash to Courtney.

The money put into a business by its owners is **capital**. A business proprietor invests capital with the intention of earning profit.

When Courtney Spice sets up her business:

Capital invested   = $2,500
Cash   = $2,500

Capital is a form of liability, because it is an amount owed by the business to its owner(s). As liabilities and assets are always equal amounts, we can state the accounting equation as follows.

Assets	=	Capital	+	Liabilities

For Courtney Spice, as at 1 July 20X6:

$2,500 (cash)   = $2,500   + $0

3.2 Example continued

Courtney Spice uses some of the money invested to buy a market stall for $1,800. She also purchases some herbs and spices at a cost of $650.

This leaves $50 in cash ($2,500 – $1,800 – $650). Courtney puts $30 in the bank and keeps $20 in small change. She is now ready for her first day of market trading on 3 July 20X6.

The assets and liabilities of the business have altered. At 3 July, before trading begins, the state of her business is as follows.

Assets		=	Capital	+	Liabilities
	$				
Stall	1,800	=	$2,500	+	$0
Herbs and spices	650				
Cash at bank	30				
Cash in hand	20				
	2,500				

3.3 Example continued: profit introduced into the accounting equation

On 3 July Courtney has a very successful day. She is able to sell all of her herbs and spices for $900 cash. Courtney has sold goods costing $650 to earn revenue of $900, we can say that she has earned a profit of $250 on the day's trading.

Profits belong to the owners of a business. So the $250 belongs to Courtney and are treated as an addition to the proprietor's capital.

Assets		=	Capital		+	Liabilities
	$			$		
Stall	1,800		Original investment	2,500		
Goods – herbs and spices	0					
Cash at bank	30					
Cash in hand (20 + 900)	920		Retained profit	250		
	2,750			2,750	+	$0

3.4 Drawings

Key term

> **Drawings** are amounts taken out of a business by its owner.

Courtney Spice has made a profit of $250 from her first day's work, she may decide to draw some of the profits out of the business for living expenses. Courtney decides to take $180 from the till for herself. This $180 is not an expense to be deducted in arriving at net profit. In other words, it would be **incorrect** to calculate the net profit earned by the business as follows.

	$
Profit on sale of herbs and spices	250
Less 'wages' paid to Courtney	180
Profit earned by business (incorrect)	70

Any amounts paid by a business to its proprietor are treated by accountants as withdrawals of profit (drawings) and not as expenses incurred by the business.

In Courtney's case, the true position is that the net profit earned is the $250 surplus on sale of herbs and spices

	$
Profit earned by business	250
Less profit withdrawn by Courtney	180
Profit retained in the business	70

The drawings are taken in cash, reducing the cash assets by $180. After the withdrawals, the accounting equation would be restated.

Assets		=	**Capital**		+ **Liabilities**
	$			$	
Stall	1,800		Original investment	2,500	
Goods – herbs and spices	0		Retained profit (250 – 180)	70	
Cash at bank	30				
Cash in hand (920-180)	740				
	2,570			2,570	+ $0

Assessment focus points

> A statement of financial position balances, ie Assets = Capital + liabilities.
>
> Liabilities are what the business owes to third parties.
>
> Capital is what the business owes to its owner.
>
> Capital = Original investment *plus* profit *less* drawings.
>
> Profit = Income – expenditure.
>
> Drawings = Amounts taken out of a business by its owner.

From the above example, the accounting equation can be restated as:

Assets = Original capital + profit - drawings + liabilities.

This can be restated as:

Profit = Assets - liabilities - original capital + drawings

This format is also known as the **business equation**. This is dealt with in detail in the chapter on Incomplete records.

3.5 Example continued

The next market is on 10 July and Courtney purchases more herbs and spices for $740 cash. She is not feeling well, however, and so she accepts help for the day from her cousin Bianca, for a wage of $40. On 10 July, they sell all the goods for $1,100 cash. Courtney pays Bianca her wage of $40 and draws out $200 for herself.

Required

(a)   State the accounting equation before trading began on 10 July.

(b)   State the accounting equation at the end of 10 July, after paying Bianca

    (i)   but before drawings are taken out.

    (ii)   after drawings have been made.

The accounting equation for the business at the end of transactions for 3 July is given in section 3.4.

Solution

(a)   After the purchase of the goods for $740.

Assets		=	Capital	+	Liabilities
	$				
Stall	1,800				
Goods	740				
Cash at bank	30				
Cash in hand					
(740 – 740)	0				
	2,570	=	$ 2,570	+	$0

(b)   (i)   On 10 July after Bianca is paid $40.

Assets		=	Capital		+	Liabilities
	$			$		
Stall	1,800		At beginning of 10 July	2,570		
Goods	0		Profit earned (working)	320		
Cash at bank	30					
Cash in hand						
(0 + 1,100 – 40)	1,060					
	2,890			2,890	+	$0

Working

		$	$
Sales			1,100
Less: Cost of goods sold		740	
Bianca's wage		40	
			780
Profit earned			320

    (ii)   After Courtney has taken drawings of $200.

Assets		=	Capital		+	Liabilities
	$			$		
Stall	1,800		At beginning of 10 July	2,570		
			Retained profits			
Cash at bank	30		(320 – 200)	120		
Cash in hand						
(1,060 – 200)	860					
	2,690			2,690	+	$0

> **Tutorial note.** It is very important you should understand the principles described so far. Do not read on until you are confident that you understand the solution to this example.

What is Courtney's profit on 10 July?

A $200   C $320
B $120   D $2,690

Answer

C   Her profit is $320 (see 3.5 (b) (i) above).

3.6 Receivables and payables

Key terms

> A **payable** is a person to whom a business owes money and is therefore a liability of a business.
>
> A **receivable** is a person who owes money to the business and is therefore an asset of the business.

It is common business practice to make purchases on credit, with a promise to pay within 30 days or two months or three months from the date of the bill (or 'invoice') for the goods. For example, A buys goods costing $2,000 on credit from B. B sends A an invoice for $2,000, dated 4 March, with credit terms that payment must be made within 30 days. If A pays on 31 March, B will be a **payable of A** between 4 and 31 March for $2,000.

Just as a business might buy goods on credit, so might it sell goods to customers on credit. A customer who buys goods on credit is a **receivable**. Taking the example above, **A is a receivable of B** for $2,000 between 4 and 31 March.

3.7 Example continued

Courtney Spice's market stall continues to trade during the following week to 17 July 20X6. (See Paragraph 3.5 (b)(ii) for the situation as at the end of 10 July.)

(a)   Courtney needs more money in the business and so she makes the following arrangements.

   (i)   She invests a further $250 of her own savings.

   (ii)   She persuades her Uncle Phil to lend her $500 immediately. Uncle Phil tells her that she can repay the loan whenever she likes but, in the meantime, she must pay him interest of $5 each week at the end of the market day. They agree that it will probably be quite a long time before the loan is eventually repaid.

(b)   She decides that she can afford to buy a second hand van to pick up herbs and spices from her supplier and bring them to her stall in the market. She buys a van on credit for $700. Courtney agrees to pay for the van after 30 days' trial use.

(c)   During the week before the next market day (17 July), Courtney's Uncle Grant asks her if she could sell him some spice racks and herb chopping boards as presents for his friends. Courtney agrees and she buys what Uncle Grant wants, paying $300 in cash. Uncle Grant accepts delivery of the goods and agrees to pay $350 to Courtney for them, but he asks if she can wait until the end of the month for payment. Courtney agrees.

(d)   Courtney buys herbs and spices costing $800. Of these purchases $750 are paid for in cash, with the remaining $50 on seven days' credit. Courtney decides to use Bianca's services again as an assistant on market day, at an agreed wage of $40.

(e) On 17 July, Courtney once again sells all her goods, earning revenue of $1,250 cash. She takes out drawings of $240 for her week's work and pays Bianca $40 in cash. She will make the interest payment to her Uncle Phil the next time she sees him.

(f) Ignore any van expenses for the week, for the sake of relative simplicity.

Required

State the accounting equation

(i) After Courtney and Uncle Phil have put more money into the business and after the purchase of the van.
(ii) After the sale of goods to Uncle Grant.
(iii) After the purchase of goods for the weekly market.
(iv) At the end of the day's trading on 17 July, after drawings have been 'appropriated' out of profit.

Solution

This solution deals with each transaction one at a time in chronological order.

(i) *The addition of Courtney's extra capital and Uncle Phil's loan*

To the business, Uncle Phil is a long-term liability and, therefore, the amount owed to him is a liability of the business and not business capital.

Assets		= Capital		+ Liabilities	
	$		$		$
Stall	1,800	As at end of 10 July	2,690	Loan	500
Cash at bank and in hand (30+860+ 250+500)		Additional capital put in	250		
	1,640				
	3,440 =		2,940 +		500

The purchase of the van (cost $700) on credit.

Assets		= Capital		+ Liabilities	
	$		$		$
Stall	1,800	As at end of 10 July	2,690	Loan	500
Van	700	Additional capital	250	Payable	700
Cash at bank and in hand (30+860+ 250+500)					
	1,640				
	4,140 =		2,940 +		1,200

(ii) *The sale of goods to Uncle Grant on credit ($350) at a cost of $300 (cash)*

Assets		= Capital		+ Liabilities	
	$		$		$
Stall	1,800	As at end of 10 July	2,690	Loan	500
Van	700	Additional capital	250	Payable	700
Receivable	350	Profit on sale to Uncle Grant (350 – 300)	50		
Cash at bank and in hand (1,640 – 300)					
	1,340				
	4,190 =		2,990 +		1,200

(iii) *After the purchase of goods ($750 paid in cash and $50 on credit)*

Assets		=	Capital		+	Liabilities	
	$			$			$
Stall	1,800		As at end of 10 July	2,690		Loan	500
Van	700					Payable	
						for van	700
Goods	800		Additional capital	250		Payable	
						for goods	50
Receivable	350		Profit on sale to				
			Uncle Grant	50			
Cash at bank							
and in hand							
(1,340 – 750)	590						
	4,240	=		2,990	+		1,250

(iv) *After market trading on 17 July*

Assets		=	Capital		+	Liabilities	
	$			$			$
Stall	1,800		As at end of 10 July	2,690		Loan	500
Van	700		Additional capital	250		Payable for	
Receivable	350					van	700
Cash at bank						Payable for	
and in hand						goods	50
(590 + 1,250			Profits retained	215		Payable for	
–40 – 240)	1,560		(working)			interest	
						payment	5
	4,410			3,155			1,255

Working

	$	$
Sales		1,250
Cost of goods sold	800	
Wages	40	
Interest payable	5	
		845
Profit earned on 17 July		405
Profit on sale of goods to Uncle Grant		50
Profit for the week		455
Drawings appropriated out of profits		240
Retained profit		215

Question

The accounting equation

How would each of these transactions affect the accounting equation?

(a)   Purchasing $800 worth of inventory on credit
(b)   Paying the telephone bill $25
(c)   Selling $450 worth of inventory for $650
(d)   Paying $800 to the supplier

		$
(a)	Increase in liabilities (payables)	$800
	Increase in assets (inventory)	$800
(b)	Decrease in assets (cash)	$25
	Decrease in capital (profit)	$25
(c)	Decrease in assets (inventory)	$450
	Increase in assets (cash)	$650
	Increase in capital (profit)	$200
(d)	Decrease in liabilities (payables)	$800
	Decrease in assets (cash)	$800

4 The statement of financial position

A statement of financial position is a statement of the assets and liabilities of a business at a given moment in time.

4.1 Presentation of assets and liabilities

A statement of financial position can be presented in two ways.

- Assets in one half and capital and liabilities in the other
- Net assets in one half and capital in the other

An illustrated statement of financial position

(a) NAME OF BUSINESS
STATEMENT OF FINANCIAL POSITION AS AT (DATE)

	$
Assets (item by item)	X
	X
	X

	$
Capital	X
Liabilities (item by item)	X
	X

(b) NAME OF BUSINESS
STATEMENT OF FINANCIAL POSITION AS AT (DATE)

	$
Assets	X
Less liabilities	X
Net assets	X
Capital	X

Method (a) is the format preferred under International Financial Reporting Standards, while method (b) is the usual format under UK Standards. This Study Text generally uses method (a).

In either format, the total value in one half of the statement of financial position will equal the total value in the other half. You should understand this from the accounting equation.

Capital, liabilities and assets are usually shown in more detail in a statement of financial position. The following paragraphs give examples of this.

4.2 Capital (sole trader)

> **FAST FORWARD**
>
> Capital is what the business owes to the owner.

The proprietor's capital can be analysed into difference sources.

	$	$
Capital as at the beginning of the accounting period (ie capital 'brought forward')		X
Add additional capital introduced during the period		X
		X
Add profit earned during the period	X	
Less drawings	(X)	
Retained profit for the period		X
Capital as at the end of the accounting period (ie capital 'carried forward')		X

'Brought forward' means 'brought forward from the previous period', and **'carried forward'** means 'carried forward to the next period'. The carried forward amount at the end of one period is also the brought forward amount of the next period. The word 'down' is sometimes used instead of 'forward'.

The figure for retained profit is sometimes referred to as a **return on the owner's investment**, in the sense that a return is a reward for investment in a business.

4.3 Liabilities

> **FAST FORWARD**
>
> Liabilities are what the business owes to third parties. They represent the business's obligation to transfer economic benefits to a third party.

The various liabilities are detailed separately. A distinction is made between current liabilities and long-term liabilities.

4.4 Current liabilities

> **Key term**
>
> **Current liabilities** are debts of the business that must be paid within a fairly short period of time. By convention, a 'fairly short period of time' is taken as one year.

In the accounts of UK limited liability companies, the CA 2006 requires the use of the term 'creditors: amounts falling due within one year' rather than 'current liabilities'. However, International Financial Reporting Standards (IFRSs) use the term 'current liabilities'.

Examples of current liabilities

- Loans repayable within one year
- Bank overdraft (repayable on demand, in theory)
- Trade payables (suppliers to whom the business owes money)
- Taxation payable
- Accrued expenses (eg gas used between the date of the last bill and the end of the accounting period for which a bill has not yet been received)

Accrued expenses will be described more fully in a later chapter.

Cash (H)

$
5,00

RENT EX

$

Cash (B)

NON-CURRENT ASS

Cash (E)

SA

5 Cash boo

FAST FORWARD The **cash book** lists a

5.1 The cash b

The cash book recor
cheques into the ban

Some cash, in notes
expense. This cash is

5.2 Example: c

At the beginning of 1

During 1 September

(a) Cash sale – re
(b) Payment from
(c) Payment from
(d) Payment from
(e) Cheque receiv
(f) Second cash s
(g) Cash received
(h) Payment to su
(i) Payment to su
(j) Payment of tel
(k) Payment of ga
(l) $100 in cash
(m) Payment of $1

Solution

The receipts part of th

Date 20X7	Narrative
1 Sept	Balance
	Cash sa
	Receival
	Receival
	Receival
	Loan: Le
	Cash sal
	Sale of r
2 Sept	Balance

* 'b/d' = brought down

Sales (G)

BANK LO

Cash (J)

OTHE

Cash (K)

D

Cash (L)

If you want to make sure that this solution
ledger accounts, once as a debit and once
be ticked, with only totals left over.

There is an easier way to check that the s
called a trial balance.

Assessment focus point Remember for every debit, there must be

Key term

Key term

Key term

Key term

Key term

3 The journal

As mentioned in the last chapter, one of the books of prime entry is the journal.

> The **journal** is a record of unusual transactions. It is used to record any double entries made which do not arise from the other books of prime entry.

Whatever type of transaction is being recorded, the format of a journal entry is as follows.

Date	Debit $	Credit $
Account to be debited	X	
Account to be credited		X
(Narrative to explain the transaction)		

A narrative explanation must accompany each journal entry. It is required for audit and control, to indicate the purpose and authority of every transaction which is not first recorded in a book of prime entry.

3.1 Example: journal entries

The following is a summary of the transactions of 'Hair by Fiona Middleton'.

1 January	Put in cash of $2,000 as capital
	Purchased brushes and combs for cash $50
	Purchased hair driers from Gilroy Ltd on credit $150
30 January	Paid three months rent to 31 March $300
	Collected and paid-in takings $600
31 January	Gave Mrs Sullivan a perm, highlights etc on credit $80

Although these entries would normally go through the other books of prime entry (eg the cash book), it is good practice for you to show these transactions as journal entries.

Solution

JOURNAL

			$	$
1 January	DEBIT	Cash account	2,000	
	CREDIT	Fiona Middleton – capital account		2,000
	Initial capital introduced			
1 January	DEBIT	Brushes and combs (asset) account	50	
	CREDIT	Cash account		50
	The purchase for cash of brushes and combs as non-current assets			
1 January	DEBIT	Hair dryer asset account	150	
	CREDIT	Sundry payables account *		150
	The purchase on credit of hair driers as non-current assets			
30 January	DEBIT	Rent expense account	300	
	CREDIT	Cash account		300
	The payment of rent to 31 March			

				$	$
30 January	DEBIT	Cash account		600	
	CREDIT	Sales account			600
	Cash takings				
31 January	DEBIT	Receivables account		80	
	CREDIT	Sales account			80
	The provision of a hair-do on credit				

* *Note.* Payables who have supplied **non current assets** are included amongst sundry payables. Payables who have supplied raw materials or goods for resale are **trade payables**. It is quite common to have separate payables accounts for trade and sundry payables.

Assessment focus point

As journal entries are a good test of your double entry skills, be prepared for assessment questions that ask how you would post a transaction and then give a selection of journal entries to choose from.

3.2 The correction of errors

FAST FORWARD

The journal is commonly used to record **corrections** of **errors** that have been made in writing up the nominal ledger accounts.

There are several types of error which can occur. They are looked at in detail in a later chapter along with the way of using journal entries to correct them.

4 Posting from day books to nominal ledger accounts

FAST FORWARD

Individual transactions are recorded in day books. Day book totals are recorded in double entry in the nominal ledger.

So far in this session we have made entries in nominal ledger accounts for each individual transaction, ie each source document has been recorded by a separate debit and credit. This means that every accounts department would need a lot of people who understand the double entry system, and that nominal ledger accounts would contain a huge number of entries. These two problems are avoided by using the books of prime entry or day books (remember these are lists of similar transactions). In practice, source documents are recorded in books of prime entry, and totals are posted from them to the nominal ledger accounts.

In the previous chapter, we used the following example of four transactions entered into the sales day book.

SALES DAY BOOK

Date 20X0	Invoice	Customer	Sales ledger refs $	Total amount invoiced $	Boot sales $	Shoe sales $
Jan 10	247	Jones & Co	SL 14	105.00	60.00	45.00
	248	Smith Ltd	SL 8	86.40	86.40	
	249	Alex & Co	SL 6	31.80		31.80
	250	Enor College	SL 9	1,264.60	800.30	464.30
				1,487.80	946.70	541.10

This day book could be posted to the ledger accounts as follows.

DEBIT   Receivables account $1,487.80

CREDIT   Total sales account $1,487.80

However a total sales account is not very informative. In our example, it is better to have a 'sale of shoes' account and a 'sale of boots' account.

		$	$
DEBIT	Receivables account	1,487.80	
CREDIT	Sale of shoes account		541.10
	Sale of boots account		946.70

This is why the sales are analysed in the day book. Exactly the same reasoning lies behind the analyses kept in other books of prime entry, so that we can record it in the nominal ledger.

Question

Purchase day book

The correct posting for the total column of the purchase day book is:

A   Debit payables account
Credit purchases account

B   Debit purchases account
Credit payables account

C   Debit receivables account
Credit sales account

D   Debit sales account
Credit receivables account

Answer

B is correct.

5 The imprest system

In the last chapter, we saw how the petty cash book was used to operate the **imprest** system for petty cash. It is now time to see how the double entry works in the imprest system.

5.1 Example: the imprest system

A business starts off a cash float on 1.3.20X7 with $250. This will be a payment from cash at bank to petty cash.

DEBIT   Petty cash $250

CREDIT   Cash at bank $250

Five payments were made out of petty cash during March 20X7.

Receipts $	Date	Narrative	Total $	Payments Postage $	Travel $
250.00	1.3.X7	Cash			
	2.3.X7	Stamps	12.00	12.00	
	8.3.X7	Stamps	10.00	10.00	
	19.3.X7	Travel	16.00		16.00
	23.3.X7	Travel	5.00		5.00
	28.3.X7	Stamps	11.50	11.50	
250.00			54.50	33.50	21.00

At the end of each month (or at any other suitable interval) the total credits in the petty cash book are posted to ledger accounts. For March 20X7, $33.50 would be debited to postage account and $21.00 to travel account. The credit of $54.50 would be to the petty cash account. The cash float would need to be topped up by a payment of $54.50 from the main cash book.

			$	$
DEBIT	Petty cash		54.50	
CREDIT	Cash			54.50

The petty cash book for the month of March 20X7 will look like this.

Receipts $	Date	Narrative	Total $	Payments Postage $	Travel $
250.00	1.3.X7	Cash			
	2.3.X7	Stamps	12.00	12.00	
	8.3.X7	Stamps	10.00	10.00	
	19.3.X7	Travel	16.00		16.00
	23.3.X7	Travel	5.00		5.00
	28.3.X7	Stamps	11.50	11.50	
	31.3.X7	Balance c/d	195.50		
250.00			250.00	33.50	21.00
195.50	1.4.X7	Balance b/d			
54.50	1.4.X7	Cash			

The cash float is back up to $250 on 1.4.X7, ready for more payments to be made.

Question

Imprest

A business has a petty cash imprest of $150. During a period, expenses are paid out totalling $86. What amount is needed to top up the imprest?

A $150
B $86
C $64
D $250

Answer

B $86 – the amount of the expenses for the period.

The following is a summary of the petty cash transactions of Jockfield for May 20X2.

May	1	Received from cashier $300 as petty cash float	$
	2	Postage	18
	3	Travelling	12
	4	Cleaning	15
	7	Petrol for delivery van	22
	8	Travelling	25
	9	Stationery	17
	11	Cleaning	18
	14	Postage	5
	15	Travelling	8
	18	Stationery	9
		Cleaning	23
	20	Postage	13
	24	Delivery van 5,000 miles service	43
	26	Petrol	18
	27	Cleaning	21
	29	Postage	5
	30	Petrol	14

Required

(a) Rule up a suitable petty cash book with analysis columns for expenditure on cleaning, motor expenses, postage, stationery and travelling.

(b) Enter the month's transactions.

(c) Enter the receipt of the amount necessary to restore the imprest and carry down the balance for the commencement of the following month.

(d) State how the double entry for the expenditure is completed.

(a),(b),(c)   PETTY CASH BOOK

Receipts $	Date	Narrative	Total $	Postage $	Travelling $	Cleaning $	Stationery $	Motor $
300	May 1	Cash						
	May 2	Postage	18	18				
	May 3	Travelling	12		12			
	May 4	Cleaning	15			15		
	May 7	Petrol	22					22
	May 8	Travelling	25		25			
	May 9	Stationery	17				17	
	May 11	Cleaning	18			18		
	May 14	Postage	5	5				
	May 15	Travelling	8		8			
	May 18	Stationery	9				9	
	May 18	Cleaning	23			23		
	May 20	Postage	13	13				
	May 24	Van service	43					43
	May 26	Petrol	18					18
	May 27	Cleaning	21			21		
	May 29	Postage	5	5				
	May 30	Petrol	14					14
			286	41	45	77	26	97
286	May 31	Cash						
		Balance c/d	300					
586			586					
300	June 1	Balance b/d						

(d)   The analysis totals are posted to the relevant ledger accounts by double entry:

		$	$
DEBIT	Postage expense account	41	
DEBIT	Travelling expense account	45	
DEBIT	Cleaning expense account	77	
DEBIT	Stationery expense account	26	
DEBIT	Motor expense account	97	
CREDIT	Petty cash account		286

and

		$	$
* DEBIT	Petty cash account	286	
* CREDIT	Cash account		286

*Note that this final double entry to top up the imprest would normally be posted from the cash book payments rather than from the petty cash book.

6 The sales and purchase ledgers

FAST FORWARD

Personal accounts are not part of the double entry system. They record how much is owed by a customer or to a supplier. They are **memorandum** accounts only.

6.1 Impersonal accounts and personal accounts

The accounts in the nominal ledger (ledger accounts) give figures for the statement of financial position and income statement. They are called **impersonal** accounts. However, there is also a need for **personal** accounts (most commonly for receivables and payables) and these are contained in the sales ledger and purchase ledger.

6.2 The sales ledger (receivables ledger)

FAST FORWARD

The **sales ledger** contains separate accounts for each credit customer so that, at any time, a business knows how much it is owed by each customer.

The **sales day book** provides a chronological record of invoices sent out by a business to credit customers. For many businesses, this can involve very large numbers of invoices per day or per week. The same customer can appear in several different places in the sales day book. So at any point in time, a customer may owe money on several unpaid invoices.

A business needs to keep a record of how much money each individual credit customer owes because:

- (a) A customer might telephone and ask how much he currently owes.
- (b) It provides the information needed for statements sent to credit customers at the end of each month.
- (c) It assists the business in keeping a check on the credit position of each customer to ensure that he is not exceeding his credit limit.
- (d) Most important is the need to match payments received against invoices. If a customer makes a payment, the business must set it off against the correct invoice.

Sales ledger accounts are written up in the following way.

- (a) When entries are made in the sales day book (invoices sent out), they are recorded on the **debit side** of the relevant customer account in the sales ledger.
- (b) Similarly, when entries are made in the cash book (payments received) or in the sales returns day book, they recorded on **credit side** of the customer account.

Each customer account is given a reference or code number, the 'sales ledger reference' in the **sales day book**.

6.3 Example: a sales ledger account

ENOR COLLEGE

A/c no: SL 9

	$		$
Balance b/f	250.00		
10.1.X0 Sales – SDB 48			
(invoice no 250)	1,264.60	Balance c/d	1,514.60
	1,514.60		1,514.60
11.1.X0 Balance b/d	1,514.60		

The debit side of this personal account shows amounts owed by Enor College. When Enor pays some of the money it owes it will be entered into the cash book (receipts) and subsequently entered in the credit side of the personal account. For example, if the college paid $250 on 10.1.20X0.

ENOR COLLEGE

A/c no: SL 9

	$			$
Balance b/f	250.00	10.1.X0	Cash	250.00
10.1.X0 Sales – SDB 48				
(invoice no 250)	1,264.60	Balance c/d		1,264.60
	1,514.60			1,514.60
11.1.X0 Balance b/d	1,264.60			

6.4 The purchase ledger (payables ledger)

FAST FORWARD

The **purchase ledger** contains separate accounts for each credit supplier, so that, at any time a business knows how much it owes to each supplier.

The purchase ledger, like the sales ledger, consists of a number of personal accounts. These are separate accounts for each individual supplier and they enable a business to keep a check on how much it owes each supplier.

The purchase invoice is recorded in the purchases day book. Then the purchases day book is used to update accounts in the purchase ledger.

6.5 Example: purchase ledger account

COOK & CO

A/c no: PL 31

	$		$
Balance c/d	515.00	Balance b/f	200.00
		15 Mar 20X8	
		Invoice received	
		PDB 37	315.00
	515.00		515.00
		16 March 20X8	
		Balance b/d	515.00

The credit side of this personal account shows amounts owing to Cook & Co. If the business paid Cook & Co some money, it would be entered into the cash book (payments) and subsequently be posted to the debit side of the personal account. For example, if the business paid Cook & Co $100 on 15 March 20X8.

COOK & CO

A/c no: PL 31

		$			$
15.3.X8	Cash	100.00	15.3.X8	Balance b/f	200.00
			15.3.X8	Invoice received	
	Balance c/d	415.00		PDB 37	315.00
		515.00			515.00
			16.3.X8	Balance b/d	415.00

The roles of the sales day book and purchases day book are very similar, with one book dealing with invoices sent out and the other with invoices received. The sales ledger and purchase ledger also serve similar purposes, with one consisting of personal accounts for credit customers and the other consisting of personal accounts for credit suppliers.

At 1 May 20X3 amounts owing to Omega by his customers in respect of their April purchases were:

	$
Alpha	210
Beta	1,040
Gamma	1,286
Delta	279
Epsilon	823

The amounts owing by Omega to his suppliers at 1 May were.

	$
Zeta	2,173
Eta	187
Theta	318

Transactions made by Omega during May were listed in the day books as follows.

Sales day book

	$
Gamma	432
Epsilon	129
Beta	314
Epsilon	269
Alpha	88
Delta	417
Epsilon	228
	1,877

Purchase day book

	$
Eta	423
Zeta	268
Eta	741
	1,432

Sales returns day book

	$
Epsilon	88

Cash book payments

	$
Eta	187
Theta	318
Zeta	1,000
	1,505

Cash book receipts

	$
Beta	1,040
Delta	279
Gamma	826
Epsilon	823
	2,968

Required

(a)   Open accounts for Omega's customers and suppliers and record therein the 1 May balances.
(b)   Record the transactions in the appropriate personal account and nominal ledger accounts.
(c)   Balance the personal accounts where necessary.
(d)   Extract a list of receivables at 31 May.

Answer

SALES LEDGER

(a),(b),(c)

ALPHA

	$		$
Opening balance	210		
May sales	88	Balance c/d	298
	298		298

BETA

	$		$
Opening balance	1,040	Cash	1,040
May sales	314	Balance c/d	314
	1,354		1,354

GAMMA

	$		$
Opening balance	1,286	Cash	826
May sales	432	Balance c/d	892
	1,718		1,718

DELTA

	$		$
Opening balance	279	Cash	279
May sales	417	Balance c/d	417
	696		696

EPSILON

	$		$
Opening balance	823	Cash	823
May sales	129	Returns	88
May sales	269	Balance c/d	538
May sales	228		
	1,449		1,449

PURCHASES LEDGER

ZETA

	$		$
Cash	1,000	Opening balance	2,173
Balance c/d	1,441	May purchases	268
	2,441		2,441

ETA

	$		$
Cash	187	Opening balance	187
Balance c/d	1,164	May purchases	423
		May purchases	741
	1,351		1,351

THETA

	$		$
Cash	318	Opening balance	318

NOMINAL LEDGER

SALES ACCOUNT

	$		$
		May sales	1,877

PURCHASES ACCOUNT

	$		$
May purchases	1,432		

SALES RETURNS ACCOUNT

	$		$
May returns	88		

RECEIVABLES ACCOUNT

	$		$
Opening balance	3,638	May returns	88
May sales	1,877	May receipts	2,968
		Balance c/d	2,459
	5,515		5,515

PAYABLES ACCOUNT

	$		$
May payments	1,505	Opening balance	2,678
		May purchases	1,432

CASH ACCOUNT

	$		$
May receipts	2,968	May payments	1,505

(d)   RECEIVABLES AS AT 31 MAY

	May
	$
Alpha	298
Beta	314
Gamma	892
Delta	417
Epsilon	538
	2,459

Note. Compare this total to the balance on the receivables account! We will return to this in the Chapter on control accounts. However you should not be surprised that the total of the individual customer accounts in the sales ledger agrees to the balance on the receivables account.

6.6 Summary

(a)   Business transactions are recorded on source documents.

(b)   Source documents are recorded in day books.

(c)   Totals of day books are recorded by double entry in nominal ledger accounts.

(d)   Single transactions are recorded from day books to individual customer and supplier accounts by single entry.

(e)   Customer accounts are in the sales ledger

(f)   Supplier accounts are in the purchase ledger

(g)   The sales and purchase ledger are not part of the double entry system

(h)   The nominal ledger contains one account for each item in the statement of financial position and income statement.

Chapter roundup

- The nominal ledger contains a separate account for each item which appears in a statement of financial position or income statement.

- The double entry system of bookkeeping means that for every debit there is an equal credit. This is sometimes referred to as the concept of duality.

- Cash transactions are settled immediately. Credit transactions give rise to receivables and payables.

- The journal is commonly used to record corrections of errors that have been made in writing up the nominal ledger accounts.

- Individual transactions are recorded in day books. Day book totals are recorded in double entry in the nominal ledger.

- Personal accounts are not part of the double entry system. They record how much is owed by a customer or to a supplier. They are memorandum accounts only.

- The sales ledger contains separate accounts for each credit customer so that, at any time, a business knows how much it is owed by each customer.

- The purchase ledger contains separate accounts for each credit supplier, so that, at any time a business knows how much it owes to each supplier.

1   The suppliers personal accounts will appear in which of the following business records?

    A   The nominal ledger
    B   The sales ledger
    C   The purchase day book
    D   The purchase ledger

2   The double entry to record a cash sale of $50 is.

    DEBIT   _____ $50

    CREDIT   _____ $50

3   The double entry to record a purchase of office chairs for $1,000 is:

    DEBIT   _____ $1,000

    CREDIT   _____ $1,000

4   The double entry to record a credit sale is:

    DEBIT   _____

    CREDIT   _____

5   Which of these statements are correct?

    (i)   The purchase day book is part of a double entry system.
    (ii)   The purchase ledger is part of a double entry system.

    A   (i) only
    B   (i) and (ii)
    C   (ii) only
    D   Both are false

6   Personal accounts contain records of

    A   Receivables and payables
    B   Assets and liabilities
    C   Income and expenditure
    D   Transactions with the proprietor of the business

7   A credit sale of $2,000 would be recorded using which of the following journals?

    A   DEBIT sales $2,000
            CREDIT receivables $2,000

    B   DEBIT receivables $2,000
            CREDIT sales $2,000

    C   DEBIT sales ledger $2,000
            CREDIT sales $2,000

    D   DEBIT sales $2,000
            CREDIT sales ledger $2,000

Answer

First you must pι

Account

Bank loan
Cash
Capital
Rent
Trade payabloc
Purchases
Sales
Sundry payables
Receivables
Bank loan interes
Other expenses
Vehicles

Now we must tak

(a) DEBIT
     CREDIT

(b) DEBIT

     CREDIT

(c) DEBIT
     CREDIT

When these figur

Account

Bank loan
Cash (11,700 – 5·
Capital
Rent
Trade payables (1
Purchases (12,40
Sales (14,600 + 1
Sundry payables
Receivables (12,0
Bank loan interes
Other expenses (
Vehicles

And it balances!

Answers to quick quiz

1   D   This is correct
    A   This ledgers is used to record impersonal accounts.
    B   Customers accounts are kept in the sales ledger.
    C   This is simply a record of purchase invoices received.

2   DEBIT: CASH $50; CREDIT: SALES $50

3   DEBIT: NON-CURRENT ASSETS $1,000; CREDIT: CASH $1,000

4   DEBIT: RECEIVABLES; CREDIT: SALES

5   D is correct. The purchase day book is a book of prime entry, and the purchase ledger shows balances on suppliers accounts. Neither are part of the double entry in the nominal ledger.

6   A   Correct.
    B   These would be in the nominal ledger.
    C   These would be in the nominal ledger.
    D   These would be in either the nominal ledger or a 'private ledger' not accessible by accounting staff.

7   B   Correct.
    A   This is a reversal of the correct entries.
    C&D   Remember that the sales ledger is not usually part of the double entry system.

Now try the questions below from the Question Bank

Question numbers
13–19

FAST FORWARD

FAST FORWARD

Assessment focus point

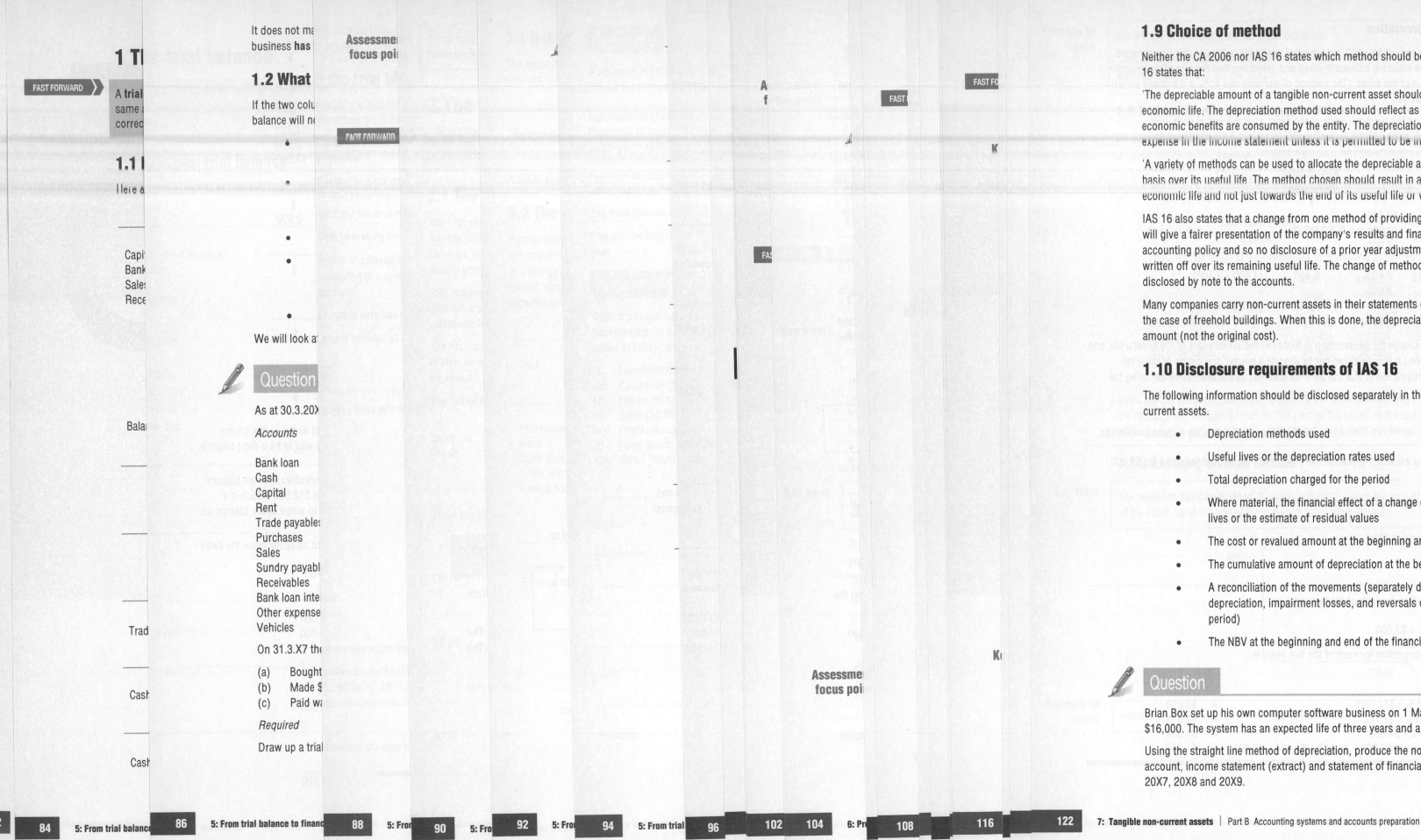

1 T...

FAST FORWARD

A **trial**
same
correc...

1.1 ...

Here a...

Capi...
Bank
Sales
Rece...

Bala...

Trad...

Cash...

Cash...

It does not ma...
business **has**...

Assessme
focus poi...

1.2 What...

If the two colu...
balance will n...

FAST FORWARD

We will look a...

Question

As at 30.3.20X...

Accounts

Bank loan
Cash
Capital
Rent
Trade payables
Purchases
Sales
Sundry payabl...
Receivables
Bank loan inte...
Other expense...
Vehicles

On 31.3.X7 th...

(a)   Bought...
(b)   Made $...
(c)   Paid wa...

Required

Draw up a trial...

Assessme
focus poi

1.9 Choice of method

Neither the CA 2006 nor IAS 16 states which method should be use...
16 states that:

'The depreciable amount of a tangible non-current asset should be...
economic life. The depreciation method used should reflect as fairly...
economic benefits are consumed by the entity. The depreciation ch...
expense in the income statement unless it is permitted to be includ...

'A variety of methods can be used to allocate the depreciable amou...
basis over its useful life. The method chosen should result in a **dep**...
economic life and not just towards the end of its useful life or whe...

IAS 16 also states that a change from one method of providing dep...
will give a fairer presentation of the company's results and financ...
accounting policy and so no disclosure of a prior year adjustment i...
written off over its remaining useful life. The change of method, the...
disclosed by note to the accounts.

Many companies carry non-current assets in their statements of fir...
the case of freehold buildings. When this is done, the depreciation...
amount (not the original cost).

1.10 Disclosure requirements of IAS 16

The following information should be disclosed separately in the fin...
current assets.

- Depreciation methods used

- Useful lives or the depreciation rates used

- Total depreciation charged for the period

- Where material, the financial effect of a change durin...
  lives or the estimate of residual values

- The cost or revalued amount at the beginning and en...

- The cumulative amount of depreciation at the beginn...

- A reconciliation of the movements (separately disclo...
  depreciation, impairment losses, and reversals of pa...
  period)

- The NBV at the beginning and end of the financial pe...

Question

Brian Box set up his own computer software business on 1 March...
$16,000. The system has an expected life of three years and a resi...

Using the straight line method of depreciation, produce the non-cu...
account, income statement (extract) and statement of financial pos...
20X7, 20X8 and 20X9.

An alternative method of calculation is

Normal' depreciation charge per annum
Further fall in value, from net book value at end of yea
Charge against profit in year 5

The leasehold has a further 15 years to run and its va
depreciation will be

$$\frac{\$60,000}{15 \text{ years}} = \$4,000 \text{ per annum}$$

Question

PS acquired its premises on 1 January 20X4 at a cos

Buildings
Land

The depreciation policy of the company is to write of
straight-line method and assuming a nil residual val

On 1 January 20X9 the buildings and land were reva

Buildings
Land

Required

Calculate the following.

(i)   The net book value of land and buildings at 3
(ii)   The net book value of land and buildings at 3
(iii)   The capital reserve at 31 December 20X9

Answer

(i)   **Valuation of land and buildings at 31 Dece**

Buildings (a finite life asset)
Depreciation
$140,000 ÷ 25 years = $5,600 pa
$5,600 × 5 years

Land (an infinite asset)

(ii)   **Valuation of land and buildings at 31 Dece**

Buildings at valuation
Depreciation
$200,000 ÷ 20 years

Land

After five years, on 1 January 20X6, the business premise

Land
Building

He estimates that the building still has a further 25 years of usefi

Calculate the annual charge for depreciation in each of the 30 ye
value of the land and building as at the end of each year.

Solution

Before the revaluation, the annual depreciation charge is $1,00(
made in each of the first five years of the asset's life.

The net book value of the total asset will decline by $1,000 per a

(a) $49,000 as at 31.12.X1
(b) $48,000 as at 31.12.X2
(c) $47,000 as at 31.12.X3
(d) $46,000 as at 31.12.X4
(e) $45,000 as at 31.12.X5

When the revaluation takes place, the amount of the revaluatio

New asset value
Net book value as at end of 20X5
Amount of revaluation

The asset will be revalued by $105,000 to $150,000. If you reme
assets go up in value by $105,000, capital or liabilities must inc
benefits the owner of the business, the amount of the revaluatio
reserve.

After a revaluation, depreciation is calculated using the following

$$\frac{\text{Revalued amount} - \text{residual value (if any)}}{\text{Remaining useful life}}$$

After the revaluation, depreciation will be charged on the buildi

$$\frac{\$75,000}{25 \text{ years}} = \$3,000 \text{ per annum}$$

The net book value of the property will then fall by $3,000 per a
20X6 to only $75,000 at the end of the 25 years – ie the building

The consequence of an upwards revaluation is therefore a highe

2.3 Revaluation method of depreciation

Under the revaluation method of depreciation, an asset is revalu
two amounts is then taken as depreciation.

Answer

NON-CURRENT ASSET – COMPUTER EQUIPMENT

	Date		$	Date		$
(a)	1.3.X6	Payable	16,000	28.2.X7	Balance c/d	16,000
(b)	1.3.X7	Balance b/d	16,000	28.2.X8	Balance c/d	16,000
(c)	1.3.X8	Balance b/d	16,000	28.2.X9	Balance c/d	16,000
(d)	1.3.X9	Balance b/d	16,000			

The non-current asset has now lasted its expected useful life. However, until it is sold or scrapped, the asset still appears in the statement of financial position at cost (less accumulated depreciation) and it remains in the ledger account for computer equipment until disposal.

PROVISION FOR DEPRECIATION

	Date		$	Date		$
(a)	28.2.X7	Balance c/d	4,500	28.2.X7	I/S	4,500
(b)	28.2.X8	Balance c/d	9,000	1.3.X7	Balance b/d	4,500
				28.2.X8	I/S	4,500
			9,000			9,000
(c)	28.2.X9	Balance c/d	13,500	1.3.X8	Balance b/d	9,000
				28.2.X9	I/S	4,500
			13,500			13,500
				1 Mar 20X9	Balance b/d	13,500

The annual depreciation charge is $\frac{(\$16,000 - 2,500)}{3 \text{ years}} = \$4,500 \text{ pa}$

The asset is depreciated to its residual value. If it continues to be used, it will not be depreciated any further (unless its residual value is reduced).

INCOME STATEMENT (EXTRACT)

	Date		$
(a)	28 Feb 20X7	Provision for depreciation	4,500
(b)	28 Feb 20X8	Provision for depreciation	4,500
(c)	28 Feb 20X9	Provision for depreciation	4,500

STATEMENT OF FINANCIAL POSITION (EXTRACT) AS AT 28 FEBRUARY

	20X7	20X8	20X9
	$	$	$
Computer equipment at cost	16,000	16,000	16,000
Less accumulated depreciation	4,500	9,000	13,500
Net book value	11,500	7,000	2,500

However a business can depreciate different categories of non[...]
cars, then each car is depreciated in the same way (eg the stra[...]
asset (photocopiers) can be depreciated using a different met[...]

1.15 Changes in residual value or remainin[...]

If there is a change in residual value or remaining useful life, [...]

Net book value − revised residual value (if any)
──
                Revised useful life

Assessment
focus point

(a)   Depreciation is a measure of the 'wearing out' of a non[...]

(b)   The accruals concept requires that depreciation be cha[...]

(c)   Two common methods of calculating depreciation are [...]

(d)   To record depreciation:

       DEBIT   Depreciation expense account
       CREDIT   Depreciation provision

       Then to get the charge into the income statement

       DEBIT   Income statement
       CREDIT   Depreciation expense account

Assessment
focus point

2 Revaluation of non-current ass[...]

FAST FORWARD

When a non-current asset is revalued, depreciation is charge[...]

2.1 Revaluations

Due to inflation, it is now quite common for the market value [...]
example of rising market values is land and buildings.

A business is not obliged to revalue non-current assets. How[...]
revalue some non-current assets upwards. When non-curren[...]
revalued amount.

2.2 Example: the revaluation of non-curre[...]

Ira Vann commenced trading on 1 January 20X1 and purcha[...]

For the purpose of accounting for depreciation, he decided t[...]

(a)   the freehold land part of the business premises was [...]

(b)   the building part of the business premises was worth [...]
       straight-line method to a nil residual value over 30 ye[...]

Question

A machine is revalued at the end of the financial y[...]
valued at $250,000. Historical cost was $280,000[...]
method in the income statement?

A $40,000
B $30,000
C $10,000
D $20,000

Answer

C   Over the course of the year the machine's [...]

2.4 A fall in the value of a non-cu[...]

When the 'market' value of a non-current asset f[...]
permanent, the asset is written down to its new [...]
the value of the asset during the accounting peri[...]

Net book value at the beginning of the period
Less: new value
Equals: the charge for the impairment in the ass[...]

However, if the asset has been previously revalu[...]

Assessment
focus point

Impairment in this case is different to the revalu[...]
carried out every 2 or 3 years. It is not a method[...]

2.5 Example: fall in asset value

A business purchased a leasehold property on [...]
years' use, on 1 January 20X6, the leasehold is [...]

Solution

Before the asset is reduced in value, the annua[...]

$$\frac{\$100,000}{20\ years} = \$5,000\ per\ annum\ (= 5\%\ of\ \$100,0[...]$$

After 5 years, the accumulated depreciation is [...]
new asset value. This $15,000 is written off in [...]

Net book value of the leasehold after 4 years ([...]
Revised asset value at end of year 5
Charge against profit in year 5

FAST FORWARD

Key term

1   Cost of sales is calculated as _____
    _____. (Fill in the blanks.)

2   Carriage inwards reduces gross profit and net profit. True or fa

3   Carriage outwards reduces gross profit and net profit. True or

4   Carriage inwards is added to cost of sales because

    A   It is an expense of the business
    B   It is an expense connected with purchasing stock for re
    C   It is not a controllable expense of running the business
    D   If it appeared in the income and expenditure account, ne

5   Put debit or credit in the blanks.

    Closing inventory is a _____ in the statement
    in the trading account.

6   Net realisable value is _____
    _____

7   IAS 2 requires inventory to be valued using a consistent approa
    the correct approach?

    A   At the higher of cost or net realisable value
    B   At cost
    C   At net realisable value
    D   At the lower of cost or net realisable value

8   IAS 2 requires inventory to be valued using acceptable methods

    Which of the following is an unacceptable method of valuing inv

    A   'First in First out'
    B   'Average cost'
    C   'Last in First out'
    D   Standard cost

9   At the year end a business has inventories of bags and bells.

    Original purchase price (per unit)
    Number in stock
    Estimated future sales price (per unit)
    Estimated selling costs (per unit)

    The value of closing inventory is $_____.

The profit differences are only temporary. In our example, the opening inventory in December 20X2 will be $6,000, $5,874 or $5,700, depending on the inventory valuation used. Different opening inventory values will affect the cost of sales and profits in December, so that in the long run inequalities in costs of sales each month will even themselves out.

Question

Inventory valuation

In times of inflation, changing from a FIFO method of inventory valuation to a LIFO method is likely to:

A   Increase reported profit
B   Reduce reported profit
C   Have no effect on reported profit
D   Have an unpredictable effect on reported profit

Answer

B is correct. Under FIFO, inventory was the most recent purchases. Under LIFO, inventory is the oldest (and cheapest) purchases. Thus, changing to LIFO puts up the cost of sales and reduces reported profits.

Chapter roundup

- The accruals concept requires us to match income with the
  unsold at the end of an accounting period and so still be he
  be included in the cost of sales of the period.

- The cost of goods sold is calculated by adding the value of
  the value of closing inventory.

- Carriage inwards is part of 'purchases'. Carriage outwards i

- Businesses must account accurately for inventory. Inventor
  must be known in order to compute **cost of sales**.

- The value of closing inventories is accounted for in the nor
  trading account at the end of an accounting period. At the b
  value b/f in the inventory account is transferred to the tradi

- The quantity of inventories held at the year end is establishe
  inventory count exercise, or by a 'continuous' inventory cou

- Inventory is valued in accordance with the prudence concep
  comprises purchase costs and costs of conversion.

- Net realisable value is the selling price less all costs to com

- The possible methods of valuing inventories include FIFO, L
  Financial accounts will normally require the use of FIFO or a

---

(c) Sales tax on expenses incurred on domestic accommodation for directors.

(d) Sales tax on non-business items passed through the business accounts with limited relief where the goods are used partly in the business.

(e) Sales tax which does not relate to the making of supplies in the course of a business.

> **FAST FORWARD**
>
> Where sales tax is not recoverable, for any of the reasons described above, it must be regarded as part of the cost of the items purchased and included in the I/S charge or in the statement of financial position as appropriate.

1.5 Relief for bad debts

Relief is available for sales tax on bad debts if the debt is over six months old (measured from the date of the supply) and has been written off in the payable's accounts. Where a supplier of goods or services has accounted for sales tax on the supply and the customer does not pay, the supplier may claim a refund of sales tax on the amount unpaid.

Where payments on account have been received, they are attributed to debts in date order. The consideration must be money and ownership of goods must have passed.

If the customer later pays all or part of the amount owed, a corresponding part of the sales tax repaid must be paid back to the tax authorities.

In order to claim the relief, the supplier must have a copy of the tax invoice and records to show that the sales tax has been accounted for and the debt has been written off. The sales tax is reclaimed on the payable's sales tax return.

2 Accounting for sales tax

> **FAST FORWARD**
>
> Registered businesses charge output sales tax on sales and suffer input sales tax on purchases. Sales tax does not affect the income statement, but is simply being collected on behalf of the tax authorities to whom a quarterly payment is made.

2.1 Income statement

A business does not make any profit out of the sales tax it charges. It therefore follows that its income statement figures should not include sales tax. For example, if a business sells goods for $600 + sales tax $105, ie for $705 total price, the sales account should only record the $600 excluding sales tax. The accounting entries to record the sale would be as follows.

DEBIT	Cash or trade receivables	$705
CREDIT	Sales	$600
CREDIT	Sales tax payable (output sales tax)	$105

(a) If input sales tax is recoverable, the cost of purchases should exclude the sales tax and be recorded net of tax. For example, if a business purchases goods on credit for $400 + sales tax $70, the transaction would be recorded as follows.

DEBIT	Purchases	$400
DEBIT	Sales tax payables (input sales tax recoverable)	$70
CREDIT	Trade payables	$470

(b) If the input sales tax is not recoverable, the cost of purchases must include the tax, because it is the business itself which must bear the cost of the tax.

	Purchases	Sales
Income statement	Irrecoverable input sales tax: include	Exclude sales tax
	Recoverable input sales tax: exclude	

2.2 Sales tax in the cash book, sales day book and purchase day book

When a business makes a credit sale the total amount invoiced, including sales tax, will be recorded in the sales day book. The analysis columns will then separate the sales tax from the sales income of the business as follows.

Date	Total	Sales income	Sales tax
	$	$	$
A Detter and Sons	235	200	35

When a business is invoiced by a supplier the total amount payable, including sales tax, will be recorded in the purchase day book. The analysis columns will then separate the recoverable input sales tax from the net purchase cost to the business as follows.

Date	Total	Purchase	Sales tax
	$	$	$
A Splier (Merchants)	188	160	28

When receivables pay what they owe, or payables are paid, there is **no need to show** the sales tax in an analysis column of the cash book, because input and output sales tax arise when the sale is made, not when the debt is settled.

The standard rate of VAT in the UK is 20%. However the CIMA examiners use a variety of rates including 15% and 17.5%, therefore you should use the rate of sales tax given in the question.

However, sales tax charged on **cash sales** or sales tax paid on **cash purchases** will be analysed in a separate column of the cash book. This is because output sales tax has just arisen from the cash sale and must be credited to the sales tax payables in the ledger accounts. Similarly input sales tax paid on cash purchases, having just arisen, must be debited to the sales tax payable.

For example, the receipts side of a cash book might be written up as follows.

Date	Narrative	Total	Analysis columns		
			Sales ledger	Cash sales	Output sales tax on cash sales
		$	$	$	$
	A Detter & Sons	235	235		
	Owen	660	660		
	Cash sales	329		280	49
	Newgate Merchants	184	184		
	Cash sales	94		80	14
		1,502	1,079	360	63

The payments side of a cash book might be written up as follows.

Date	Narrative	Total	Purchase ledger	Analysis columns	Input sales tax on cash purchases
				Cash purchases and sun-dry items	
		$	$	$	$
	A Splier (Merchants)	188	188		
	Telephone bill paid	141		120	21
	Cash purchase of stationery	47		40	7
	Sales tax paid to tax authorities	1,400		1,400	
		1,776	188	1,560	28

Question

Are trade receivables and trade payables shown in the accounts inclusive of sales tax or exclusive of sales tax?

Answer

They are shown **inclusive** of sales tax, as the statement of financial position must reflect the total amount due from receivables and due to payables.

Assessment focus point

A small element of sales tax is quite likely in questions. It is worth spending a bit of time ensuring that you understand the logic behind the way sales tax is accounted for, rather than trying to learn the rules by rote. This will ensure that even if you forget the rules, you will be able to work out what should be done.

2.3 Payable for sales tax

FAST FORWARD

An outstanding payable for sales tax will appear as a current liability in the statement of financial position.

The sales tax paid to the authorities each quarter is the difference between recoverable input sales tax on purchases and output sales tax on sales. For example, if a business is invoiced for input sales tax of $8,000 and charges sale tax of $15,000 on its credit sales and sales tax of $2,000 on its cash sales, the sales tax payable account would be as follows.

SALES TAX PAYABLE

	$		$
Payables (input sales tax)	8,000	Receivables (output sales tax invoiced)	15,000
Cash (payment to authorities)	9,000	Cash (output sales tax on cash sales)	2,000
	17,000		17,000

Payments to the authorities do not coincide with the end of the accounting period of a business, and so at the reporting date there will be a balance on the sales tax payable account. If this balance is for an amount payable to the authorities, the outstanding payable for sales tax will appear as a current liability in the statement of financial position.

Occasionally, a business will be owed money back by the authorities, and in such a situation, the sales tax refund owed by the authorities would be a current asset in the statement of financial position.

Question

A business in its first period of trading charges $4,000 of sales tax on its sales and suffers $3,500 of sales tax on its purchases which include $250 sales tax on business entertaining. Prepare the sales tax payable account.

Answer

SALES TAX PAYABLE ACCOUNT

	$		$
Payables	3,250	Receivables	4,000
Balance c/d (owed to tax authorities)	750		
	4,000		4,000
		Balance b/d	750

The main points

(a) Credit sales

(i) Include sales tax in sales day book; show it

(ii) Include gross receipts from receivables in cashbook; no need to show sales tax separately

(iii) Exclude sales tax element from income statement

(iv) Credit sales tax payable with output sales tax element of receivables invoiced

(b) Credit purchases

(i) Include sales tax in purchases day book; show it separately

(ii) Include gross payments in cashbook; no need to show sales tax separately

(iii) Exclude recoverable sales tax from income statement

(iv) Include irrecoverable sales tax in income statement

(v) Debit sales tax payable with recoverable input sales tax element of credit purchases

(c) Cash sales

(i) Include gross receipts in cashbook; show sales tax separately

(ii) Exclude sales tax element from income statement

(iii) Credit sales tax payable with output sales tax element of cash sales

(d) Cash purchases

(i) Include gross payments in cashbook: show sales tax separately

(ii) Exclude recoverable sales tax from income statement

(iii) Include irrecoverable sales tax in income statement

(iv) Debit sales tax payable with recoverable input sales tax element of cash purchases

Chapter roundup

- **Sales tax** is an indirect tax levied on the sale of goods and services. It is administered by the tax authorities.

- If output sales tax exceeds input sales tax, the business pays the difference in tax to the authorities. If output sales tax is less than input sales tax in a period, the tax authorities will refund the difference to the business.

- Where sales tax is not recoverable, for any of the reasons described above, it must be regarded as part of the cost of the items purchased and included in the I/S charge or in the statement of financial position as appropriate.

- Registered businesses charge output sales tax on sales and suffer input sales tax on purchases. Sales tax does not affect the income statement, but is simply being collected on behalf of the tax authorities to whom a quarterly payment is made.

- An outstanding payable for sales tax will appear as a current liability in the statement of financial position.

Quick quiz

1   Sales tax is:

   A   A direct tax levied on sales of goods and services
   B   An indirect tax levied on the sales of goods and services
   C   Administered by the Treasury
   D   Charged by businesses on taxable supplies

2   What are the two rates of sales tax which may be applicable to taxable outputs?

   (1)   _____

   (2)   _____

3   When sales tax is not recoverable on the cost of a motor car, it should be treated in which of the following ways?

   A   Deducted from the cost of the asset capitalised
   B   Included in the cost of the asset capitalised
   C   Deducted from output tax for the period
   D   Written off to I/S as an expense

4   Purchases of goods costing $500 subject to sales tax at 17.5% occur. Which of the following correctly records the **credit purchase**?

   A   Dr   Purchases $500.00
        Dr   Sales tax $87.50
        Cr   Payables $587.50

   B   Dr   Purchases $587.50
        Cr   Payables $587.50

   C   Dr   Purchases $412.50
        Dr   Sales tax $87.50
        Cr   Payables $500.00

   D   Dr   Purchases $500.00
        Cr   Sales tax $87.50
        Cr   Payables $412.50

accounting period ended 28 February 20
statement of financial position of the Sq

In the same way, there was a prepaymer
at 28 February 20X7.

Summary

Prepaid insurance premiums as at 28 Fe
Add insurance premiums paid 1 June 20

Less insurance costs charged to the I/S
Equals prepaid insurance premiums as a

Question

The Batley Print Shop rents a photocopyi

* Three months rental in advance
* A further charge of 2 pence per co

The rental agreement began on 1 August

Bills dated and received

1 August 20X4
1 November 20X4
1 February 20X5
1 May 20X5
1 August 20X5
1 November 20X5

The bills are paid promptly, as soon as th

(a) Calculate the charge for photocopy
    and/or accrued charges as at that

(b) Calculate the charge for photocopy
    prepayments and/or accrued charg

Answer

(a) Year to 31 August 20X4

    One months' rental (1/3 × $2,100)
    Accrued copying charges (1/3 × $1
    Photocopying expense (I/S)

    * From the quarterly bill dated
    ** From the quarterly bill dated

    There is a prepayment for 2 months
    20X4.

The double entry will be **reversed** i
expense (accruals) *or* will never ch
postings for the example in 1.4.

20X2
30.4   Cash
31.7   Cash
31.10   Cash
31.12   Balance c/d (accrual)

20X3
31.1   Cash
30.4   Cash
31.7   Cash
31.10   Cash
31.12   Balance c/d (accrual)

The income statement charge and

Invoice paid
31.1.X3   6,491.52
30.4.X3   5,400.94
31.7.X3   4,700.94
31.10.X3   4,620.00
31.1.X4   6,753.24
Charge to I/S in 20X3

In the example in paragraph 2.1 it
payments in 20X3, and the balanc

Assessment focus point

Don't worry too much about the ic
forward to the next period.

Question

Ratsnuffer deals in pest control. It
the year to 31 December 20X5. At

On 1 July 20X6, he hired a trainee

He pays his work force on the firs
their salary for January on the firs

Required

(a) Calculate the cost of salari
(b) Calculate the amount actua
(c) State the amount of accrue

Solution

The telephone expenses for the year e

1 March – 31 March 20X6 (no teleph
1 April – 30 June 20X6
1 July – 30 September 20X6
1 October – 31 December 20X6
1 January – 28 February 20X7 (two r

The charge for the period 1 January –
February 20X7, no telephone bill has
to ignore the telephone expenses for

The accrued charge will also appear i
current liability.

1.4 Example: accruals

Cleverley started in business as a pap
December 20X2. Electricity bills recei

31 January
30 April
31 July
31 October

What should the electricity charge be

Solution

The three invoices received during 20
and December electricity charge was
necessary to **accrue** the charge for N

Paid in year
Accrual ($^2/_3$ × $6,491.52)

The double entry for the accrual (usir

DEBIT   Electricity
CREDIT   Accruals (

2 Prepayments

Key term

Prepayments are payments which ha
until a later period, because they rela

Assessment focus point

Accruals are current liabilities and pr

Acc
prep

Introc

Profit is the
much incor
purpose of

We shall co
feature is th
Chapter 6.

Topic list

Topic list
1 Accruals
2 Prepaym
3 Accounti

---

5   A business purchases goods valued at $400. Sales tax is charged at 17.5%. The double entry to record the purchase is:

    DEBIT   _____ $_____

    DEBIT   _____ $_____

    CREDIT   _____ $_____

6   Fill in the blanks.

    Input sales tax is _____, output sales tax
    is _____.

7   When a cash sale is made for $117.50 (including sales tax) the entries made are:

    DEBIT   _____ account $_____

    CREDIT   _____ account $_____

    CREDIT   _____ account $_____

8   When a cash purchase of $117.50 is made (including sales tax) the entries are:

    DEBIT   _____ account $_____

    DEBIT   _____ account $_____

    CREDIT   _____ account $_____

9   The sales tax paid to the tax authorities each quarter is the difference between _____
    _____ and _____
    _____.

1

2

3

4

5

6

7

8

9

1 Accruals

1.1 introduction

The accruals concept says that inc
they are earned or incurred, not pa

Expenses might not be paid for dur
per annum, paid in full on 1 July ea
20X7, the correct charge for rent i
period. Similarly, the rent charge ir
period.

Accruals and prepayments can see
expenses are matched against the

Accruals and prepayments are the
period for something which relates
to the next period. If we have incu
an accrual to bring the charge bac

1.2 Accruals

Key term

Accruals or accrued expenses are
they have not yet been paid for.

Accruals are current liabilities.

1.3 Example: accruals

Horace Goodrunning, trading as G
telephone was installed on 1 April
pays it promptly as soon as it is re
charged to the income statement f

Goodrunning Motor Spares – tele

30.6.20X6
30.9.20X6
31.12.20X6
31.3.20X7

2.1 Example: prepaym

A business opens on 1 January 2
quarterly in advance. Payments w

1 January 20X4
25 March 20X4
24 June 20X4
29 September 20X4
25 December 20X4

What will the rental charge be f

Solution

The total amount paid in the yea
entirely a prepayment (give or ta
for 20X4 is therefore:

Paid in year
Prepayment

The double entry for this prepay
DEBIT   Prepayment
CREDIT   Rent accou

3 Accounting for

3.1 Double entry for a

You can see from the double e
asset or a liability account.

- **Prepayments** ar
  assets as they re

- **Accruals** are inc
  incurred but for

Transaction	DR
Accrual	Expense
Prepayment	Asset

3.2 Reversing accrua

Accruals and prepayments are

(a)   Salaries cost in the income stat

Cost of 8 employees for a full y
Cost of trainee for a half year

(b)   Salaries actually paid in 20X6

December 20X5 salaries paid in
Salaries of 8 employees for Jan
employees × $1,100 per month
Salary of trainee (for July – Nov
20X6: 5 months × $700 per mor
Salaries actually paid

(c)   Accrued salaries costs as at 31
(ie costs charged in the I/S, but

8 employees x 1 month x $1,10
1 trainee x 1 month x $700 per

(d)   Summary

Accrued wages costs as at 31 D
Add salaries cost for 20X6 (I/S)

Less salaries paid
Equals accrued wages costs as

3.3 Example: prepayments

The Square Wheels Garage pays fire ins
insurance payments, calculate the charg

1.6.20X6
1.6.20X7

Solution

Insurance cost for:

(a)   the 3 months, 1 March – 31 M
(b)   the 9 months, 1 June 20X7 – 2
Insurance cost for the year, charged to

At 28 February 20X8 there is a prepaym
insurance premium was paid on 1 June

(b)   Year to 31 August 20X5

Rental from 1 September 20X4 – 31 July 20X
$2,100 per quarter or $700 per month)
Rental from 1 August – 31 August 20X5 (1/3
Rental charge for the year
Copying charges
1 September – 31 October 20X4 (2/3 :
1 November 20X4 – 31 January 20X5
1 February – 30 April 20X5
1 May – 31 July 20X5
Accrued charges for August 20X5 (1/

Total photocopying expenses (I/S)

There is a prepayment for 2 months' rental ($
20X5.

Summary of year 1 September 20X4 – 31 Au

Prepayments as at 31.8.20X4
Accrued charges as at 31.8.20X4
Bills received during the year
1 November 20X4
1 February 20X5
1 May 20X5
1 August 20X5
Prepayment as at 31.8.20X5
Accrued charges as at 31.8.20X5
Charge to the I/S for the year
SOFP items as at 31 August 20X5
Prepaid rental (current asset)
Accrued copying charges (current liab

3.4 Further example: accruals

Willie Woggle opens a shop on 1 May 20X6. The rent
the first payment on 31 July 20X6). Willie decides tha

The rent account as at 31 December 20X6 will recor
will be two months' accrued rental expenses for Nov
period to 31 December 20X6 will be for 8 months' r

The rent account appears as follows.

RENT EXPEN

		$
20X6		
31 July	Cash	3,000
31 Oct	Cash	3,000

20X5
1 Sept   Cash

20X6
1 Jul   Balance b/d
(prepayment rev

The subscription account for th
member of the association, will

20X6
1 Jul   Balance b/d
(prepayment reve
1 Sep   Cash

20X7
1 Jul   Balance b/d
(prepayment reve

Again, we see the charge to the
will be debited to prepayments a

The allowance a...

20X2
31 Dec   Bala...

20X3
31 Dec   Bala...

For the statemen...

Sales ledger bala...
Less allowance f...

In practice, it is u...
of financial positi...
$38,000 in 20X3...

Question

Corin Flakes own...
Customers are a...
outstanding debt...

This credit syster...
operations are as...

Year to 31 Decer...
Gross profit
Bad debts writter...
Debts owed by c...
Allowance for rec...
Other expenses
Year to 31 Decer...
Gross profit
Bad debts writter...
Debts owed by c...
Allowance for rec...
Other expenses
Year to 31 Decer...
Gross profit
Bad debts writter...
Debts owed by c...
Allowance for rec...
Other expenses

Required

For each of these...
in the statement...

Required

Prepare the receivables a...

Solution

Opening balance b/f
Sales

Opening balance b/d

Receivables
Receivables

In the sales ledger, balan...
business should ensure...

1.5 Bad debts wr...

A bad debt which has be...

DEBIT   Cash acco...
CREDIT   Bad debts...

1.6 Example: bad...

An income statement for...
information.

Inventories of goods in h...
Purchases of goods
Inventories of goods in h...
Cash sales
Credit sales
Bad debts written off
Debts paid in 20X5 whic...
Other expenses

Chapter roundup

- The accruals concept says that income and expenses should be included in the income statement of the period in which they are earned or incurred, not paid or received.

- Accruals and prepayments are the means by which we move charges into the correct accounting period. If we pay in this period for something which relates to the next accounting period, we use a prepayment to transfer that charge forward to the next period. If we have incurred an expense in this period which will not be paid for until the next period, we use an accrual to bring the charge back into this period.

- Accruals and prepayments are **reversed** at the beginning of the next accounting period.

Quick quiz

1   If a business has paid rent of $1,000 for the year to 31 March 20X9, the prepayment in the accounts for the year to 31 December 20X8 is $ _____.

2   _____ in the statement of financial position are amounts incurred but not yet paid.

    _____ in the statement of financial position are amounts paid but not yet incurred.

    (Fill in the blanks.)

3   A draft income statement shows a gross profit of $2,000 and net profit of $1,000. It is then realised that $400 of rent that should be treated as a prepayment has been incorrectly treated as an accrual. When this mistake is corrected what happens to gross and net profit?

	Gross profit	Net profit
A	No change	No change
B	Falls $400	Falls $400
C	Falls $400	Rises $400
D	No change	Rises $800

4   A business pays $2,400 for a year's insurance on 1 December 20X1. The year end is 31 March 20X2. At that date, what is the balance carried forward on the insurance account?

A $800 debit
B $800 credit
C $1,600 debit
D $1,600 credit

5   A business prepares its accounts to 31 December 20X7. The trial balance includes $9,000 for electricity used from 1 January to 30 September 20X7. How much needs to be accrued at the year end?

A $9,000
B $3,000
C $6,000
D $12,000

1 Bad debts

FAST FORWARD

A **bad** debt is one that
debt will be written off.

1.1 Bad debts

Credit customers may
Customers in another
during the credit perio

1.2 Writing off

Bad debts written off a

(a)   Sales ar
earned.

(b)   Bad deb

If a sale of $300 becar

Sale
Cost of sales, say
Gross profit
Bad debt written off
Net loss on this trans

When a debt is writter

1.3 Bad debts

Bad debts written off

(a)   When a

DEBIT
CREDIT

(b)   At the e
accoun

DEBIT
CREDIT

1.4 Example: b

At 1 October 20X5 a

(a)   Credit
(b)   Payme
(c)   Two d

Assessment focus point

If dealing with
decrease in th

2.4 Exam

Alex Gullible
those balance
allowance for

On 31 Decem
that an allowa

What account
receivables w

Solution

At 31 Decem

Provision requ

Alex will make

DEBIT
CREDIT

Receivables

Sales ledger

Less allowanc

At 31 Decem

Following the

Allowance re
Existing allow
∴ Additional

He will make

DEBIT
CREDIT

Answer

AEROBIC HEALTH FOOD SHOP
INCOME STATEMENTS FOR THE YEARS ENDED 31 DECEMBER

	20X1		20X2		20X3	
	$	$	$	$	$	$
Gross profit		27,000		45,000		60,000
Reduction in allowance for receivables'						350
						60,350
Expenses:						
Bad debts written off		8,000		10,000		11,000
Increase in allowance for receivables*		1,000		250		
Other expenses		20,000		28,750		32,850
		29,000		39,000		43,850
Net(loss)/profit		(2,000)		6,000		16,500

*At 1 January 20X1 the allowance for receivables was nil. At 31 December 20X1 the allowance required was 2½% of $40,000 = $1,000. The increase in the allowance is therefore $1,000. At 31 December 20X2 the allowance required was 2½% of $50,000 = $1,250. The 20X1 allowance must therefore be increased by $250. At 31 December 20X3 the allowance required is 3% × $30,000 = $900. The 20X2 allowance is therefore reduced by $350.

Note: In practice the bad debts figure and the increase (or decrease) in the allowances for receivables are usually combined under the heading 'bad debts' in the income statement. You should be prepared for this in the assessment.

VALUE OF RECEIVABLES IN THE STATEMENT OF FINANCIAL POSITION

	As at 31.12.20X1	As at 31.12.20X2	As at 31.12.20X3
	$	$	$
Total value of receivables	40,000	50,000	30,000
Less allowance for receivables	1,000	1,250	900
SOFP value	39,000	48,750	29,100

Question

Receivables

Horace Goodrunning decides to make an allowance for receivables of 2% of outstanding receivables at the statement of financial position date from 28 February 20X6. On 28 February 20X8, Horace decides that the allowance has been over-estimated and he reduces it to 1% of outstanding receivables. Outstanding receivables balances at the various reporting dates are as follows.

	$
28.2.20X6	15,200
28.2.20X7	17,100
28.2.20X8	21,400

You are required to show extracts from the following accounts for each of the three years above.

(a)   Receivables
(b)   Allowance for receivables
(c)   Income statement

Show how receivables would appear in the statement of financial position at the end of each year.

Answer

The entries for the three years are denoted by (a), (b) and (c) in each account.

RECEIVABLES (EXTRACT)

			$		$
(a)	28.2.20X6	Balance	15,200		
(b)	28.2.20X7	Balance	17,100		
(c)	28.2.20X8	Balance	21,400		

ALLOWANCE FOR RECEIVABLES

			$				$
(a)	28.2.20X6	Balance c/d		28.2.20X6	I/S		304
		(2% of 15,200)	304				
			304				304
(b)	28.2.20X7	Balance c/d		1.3.20X6	Balance b/d		304
		(2% of 17,100)	342	28.2.20X7	I/S (note (i))		38
			342				342
(c)	28.2.20X8	I/S (note (ii))	128	1.3.20X7	Balance b/d		342
	28.2.20X8	Balance c/d					
		(1% of 21,400)	214				
			342				342
				1.3.20X8	Balance b/d		214

INCOME STATEMENT (EXTRACT)

		$
28.2.20X6	Allowance for receivables	304
28.2.20X7	Allowance for receivables	38
28.2.20X8	Allowance for receivables	(128)

Notes

(i)   The increase in the allowance is $(342 – 304) = $38
(ii)   The decrease in the allowance is $(342 – 214) = $128
(iii) We calculate the net receivables figure as follows.

	20X6	20X7	20X8
	$	$	$
Current assets			
Receivables	15,200	17,100	21,400
Less allowance for receivables	304	342	214
	14,896	16,758	21,186

2.5 Specific allowance for receivables

So far we have dealt with a general allowance for receivables. Sometimes a business may want to make an allowance against a specific receivable. If this is the case, then the general allowance is calculated on the balance of receivables after deducting the specific receivable.

2.6 Example: Specific allowance

XY Co has a balance of receivables of $250,000. It wishes to provide a specific allowance of 60% on a debt of $20,000. It also wishes to set up a general allowance of 2% of receivables. What is the charge to the income statement?

Answer

Specific allowance

$$60\% \times \$120,000 = \$12,000$$

General allowance

	$
Total receivables	250,000
Specific provision against	(20,000)
Balance	230,000

$$\text{General allowance} = 2\% \times \$230,000$$
$$= \$4,600$$

$$\text{Total allowance charged in income statement} = \$12,000 + \$4,600$$
$$= \$16,600$$

Chapter roundup

- A **bad** debt is one that is no longer expected to be paid. For instance, the customer may have gone into liquidation. This debt will be written off.

- An allowance for receivables occurs when there is uncertainty over whether a debt will be paid. The debt is not written off, but an allowance is made against non-payment.

- When an allowance is first made, the amount is charged as an expense in the income statement.

- When an allowance already exists, but is subsequently increased in size, the amount of the **increase** is charged as an expense in the income statement.

- When an allowance already exists, but is subsequently reduced in size, the amount of the **decrease** is recorded as an item of 'income' in the income statement.

Quick quiz

1   The entry to record a bad debt is:

DEBIT   _____ account

CREDIT   _____ account

2   The entry to record money received from a debt previously written off is:

DEBIT   _____ account

CREDIT   _____ account

3   The entry to record the creation of an allowance for receivables is:

DEBIT   _____ account

CREDIT   _____ account

4   The entry to record an increase in an allowance for receivables is:

DEBIT   _____ account

CREDIT   _____ account

5   Which of the fundamental accounting concepts are being applied when an allowance for receivables is set up?

A   Accruals and going concern
B   Accruals and consistency
C   Accruals and prudence
D   Going concern and prudence

6   Y has an allowance for receivables of $20,000, this is to be changed to 3% of the sales ledger balance of $500,000. Which of the following entries records the transaction?

    A   Dr   I/S a/c   } $5,000
             Cr   Receivables a/c

    B   Dr   Allowance for receivables a/c   } $5,000
             Cr   I/S a/c

    C   Dr   I/S a/c   } $5,000
             Cr   Allowance for receivables

    D   Dr   I/S a/c   } $15,000
             Cr   Allowance for receivables

Answers to quick quiz

1   DEBIT   Bad debts expense account
     CREDIT   Receivables account

2   DEBIT   Cash account
     CREDIT   Bad debts expense account

3   DEBIT   Allowance expense account
     CREDIT   Allowance for receivables account

4   DEBIT   Allowance expense account (with increase only!)
     CREDIT   Allowance for receivables account (with increase only)

5   C   This is correct because the accruals or matching concept requires bad debt expenses to be matched against related sales revenue on a prudent basis.

    A   Going concern is always presumed unless there are contrary indications.

    B   As the allowance has just been created, there are no prior year allowance against which consistency can be judged.

    D   Incorrect for reasons stated in above explanations.

6   B   Correct: the required allowance is 3% of the sales ledger balance $500,000 = $15,000. So the required reduction is $5,000, ($20,000 – $15,000).

    A   Incorrect; this entry will write off receivables balances not make an allowance.

    C   Incorrect; this entry will increase the allowance.

    D   Incorrect; this entry will increase the allowance a/c by the full amount of the allowance required.

Now try the questions below from the Question Bank

Question numbers
55–56

Bank reconciliations

Introduction

The cash book of a business is the record of how much cash the business believes that it has in the bank.

Why might the business' estimate of its bank balance be different from the amount shown on the bank statement? There are three common explanations.

(a) **Error**. Errors in calculation or recording transactions are more likely to be made by themselves than by the bank.

(b) **Bank charges or bank interest**. The bank usually only shows these on the bank statement.

(c) **Timing differences.** These include amounts banked, but not yet 'cleared' and added to the account. Similarly, payments by cheque not yet recorded by the bank.

The comparison of the cash book balance with the bank statements is called a bank reconciliation.

Topic list	Syllabus references
1 The bank reconciliation	B (1)
2 Carrying out the reconciliation	B (1)

1 The bank reconciliation

FAST FORWARD

A **bank reconciliation** is a comparison of a bank statement (sent monthly, weekly or even daily by the bank) with the cash book. Differences between the balance on the bank statement and the balance in the cash book will be errors or timing differences, and they should be identified and satisfactorily explained.

1.1 The bank statement

It is a common practice for a business to issue a monthly statement to each credit customer. In the same way, a bank sends a statement to its short-term receivables and payables – ie customers with bank overdrafts and those with money in their account – itemising the balance on the account at the beginning of the period, receipts and payments during the period, and the balance at the end of the period.

Remember, however, that if a customer has money in his account, the bank owes him that money and so the customer is a payable of the bank (hence the phrase 'to be in credit' means to have money in your account). If a business has $8,000 cash in the bank, it will have a debit balance in its own cash book, but the bank statement will show a credit balance of $8,000. (The bank's records are a 'mirror image' of the customer's own records, with debits and credits reversed.)

If you are having difficulties, think of a bank statement as a supplier's statement.

1.2 Why is a bank reconciliation necessary?

FAST FORWARD

It is important to check the cash book against the bank statement regularly. There will almost always be differences – arising from errors, omissions and timing differences.

A bank reconciliation identifies differences between the cash book and bank statement.

These can be due to:

- **Errors** – errors in the cash book or errors made by the bank

- **Bank charges** or bank interest, shown on the bank statement but not in the cash book

- **Timing differences** – items appearing in the cash book in one period but not appearing on the bank statement until a later period

Assessment focus point

A bank reconciliation is an important **control** to ensure that no unauthorised transactions go through the bank account.

1.3 What to look for when doing a bank reconciliation

The cash book and bank statement will rarely agree at a given date. When doing a bank reconciliation, you need to look for the following items.

(a) **Correction of errors**

(b) **Adjustments to the cash book**
- Payments by standing order into or from the account, not yet entered into the cash book
- Dividends received direct into the bank account, not yet entered in the cash book
- Bank interest and bank charges, not yet entered in the cash book

(c) **Timing differences reconciling the corrected cash book balance to the bank statement**

- Cheque payments credited in the cash book, not yet on the bank statement

- Cheques received, paid into the bank and debited in the cash book, but not yet on the bank statement

Key terms

Unpresented cheques are cheques sent out which do not yet appear on the statement.

Unclcarod lodgomonts are cheques received and paid into the bank which do not yet appear on the statement.

Unpresented cheques reduce the balance at the bank, uncleared lodgements increase it.

2 Carrying out the reconciliation

FAST FORWARD

When the discrepancies due to errors, omissions and timing differences are noticed, appropriate adjustments must be made. Errors must be corrected and omissions from the cash book entered. Any remaining differences should then be identified as timing differences.

2.1 Example: bank reconciliation

At 30 September 20X6, the cash book balance is $805.15 (debit). A bank statement on 30 September 20X6 shows a balance of $1,112.30.

On investigation of the difference between the two sums, the following points arise.

(a) The cash book had been undercast by $90.00 on the debit side*.
(b) Cheques paid in, not yet credited by the bank amounted to $208.20.
(c) Cheques drawn, not yet presented to the bank amounted to $425.35.

* 'Casting' is an accountant's term for adding up.

Required

(a) Show the correction to the cash book.
(b) Prepare a statement reconciling the bank statement and cash book balance.

Solution

(a)

	$
Cash book balance brought forward	805.15
Add	
Correction of undercasting	90.00
Corrected balance	895.15

(b)

	$	$
Balance per bank statement		1,112.30
Add		
Uncleared lodgements	208.20	
Less		
Unpresented cheques	425.35	
		(217.15)
Balance per cash book		895.15

Which two of the following statements are true?

(i)   Unpresented cheques should be treated as a timing difference.

(ii)   Unpresented cheques should be written back into the cash book.

(iii)   Uncleared lodgements reduce the figure per the bank statement.

(iv)   Uncleared lodgements increase the figure per bank statement.

Answer

(i) and (iv) are true.

2.2 Example: more complicated bank reconciliation

On 30 June 20X0, Cook's cash book showed an overdraft of $300 on his current account. A bank statement as at the end of June 20X0 showed that Cook was in credit with the bank by $65.

On checking the cash book with the bank statement you find the following.

(a)   Cheques drawn of $500, entered in the cash book but not yet presented.

(b)   Cheques received of $400, entered in the cash book, but not yet credited by the bank.

(c)   The bank had transferred interest received on deposit account of $60 to current account, recording the transfer on 5 July 20X0. This amount had been credited in the cash book as on 30 June 20X0.

(d)   Bank charges of $35 in the bank statement had not been entered in the cash book.

(e)   The payments side of the cash book had been undercast by $10.

(f)   Dividends received amounting to $200 were paid direct to the bank and not entered in the cash book.

(g)   A cheque for $50 drawn on deposit account had been shown in the cash book as drawn on current account.

(h)   A cheque issued to Jones for $25 was replaced when out of date. It was credited again in the cash book, no other entry being made. Both cheques were included in the total of unpresented cheques shown above.

Required

(a)   Indicate the appropriate adjustments in the cash book.

(b)   Prepare a statement reconciling the amended balance with that shown in the bank statement.

2.2 Example: I

At 1 November 20X5

PAYE control account
NIC control account
Employee savings acc

The company's wages

Total gross pay
PAYE
Employer's NIC
Employees' NIC
Employees' savings de
Net amounts paid to em

The company paid $9,3

Show the ledger accoun

Solution

PAYE control
NIC control – employee
contributions
Employee savings a/c
Bank – net pay

Bank
Balance c/d

Bank
Balance c/d

Chapt

- A ba
  cash
  timi
- It is
  arisi
- Whe
  mad
  iden

Quick

1 The
  rece

  A
  B
  C
  D

2 The
  che
  che

  A
  B
  C
  D

20X2 October		$	20X2 October	
			29	Wages
			29	Petty Cas
			29	P & Sons
		21,759		

Z BANK – STATEMENT OF ACCOUNT WITH

20X2 October		Payments $	Receipts $	
1				
1	cheque	55		
1	cheque	3,146		
1	cheque	421		O/D
2	cheque	73		
2	cheque	155		O/D
6	cheque	212		O/D
8	sundry credit		4,589	
8	cheque	3,106		
8	cheque	39		O/D
11	sundry credit		5,324	
15	sundry credit		2,313	
15	cheque	78		
15	cheque	3,029		
22	sundry credit		1,202	
22	cheque	3,217		
22	cheque	91		
25	cheque	1,782		
25	cheque	134		O/
26	cheque	929		
26	sundry credit		3,857	
26	cheque	230		
27	cheque	263		
27	cheque	77		
29	sundry credit		4,186	
29	cheque	52		
29	cheque	3,191		
29	cheque	26		
29	dividends on investments		2,728	
29	cheque	666		
31	bank charges	936		

Solution

(a) The errors to correct are given in notes (c) (e) (f) (g) and (h). Bank charges (note (d)) also need adjustment.

		Adjustments in cash book	
		Debit (ie add to cash balance)	Credit (ie deduct from cash balance)
Item		$	$
(c)	Cash book incorrectly credited with interest on 30 June, should have been debited with the receipt	60	
(c)	Debit cash book (current a/c) with transfer of interest from deposit a/c (note 1)	60	
(d)	Bank charges		35
(e)	Undercast on payments (credit) side of cash book		10
(f)	Dividends received should be debited in the cash book	200	
(g)	Cheque drawn on deposit account, not current account. Add cash back to current account	50	
(h)	Cheque paid to Jones is out of date and so cancelled. Cash book should now be debited, since previous credit entry is no longer valid (note 2)	25	
		395	45

	$	$
Cash book: balance on current account as at 30 June 20X0		(300)
Adjustments and corrections:		
Debit entries (adding to cash)	395	
Credit entries (reducing cash balance)	(45)	
Net adjustments		350
Corrected balance in the cash book		50

Notes

1 Item (c) is rather complicated. The transfer of interest from the deposit to the current account was presumably given as an instruction to the bank on or before 30 June 20X0. Since the correct entry is to debit the current account (and credit the deposit account) the correction in the cash book is to debit the current account with $2 \times \$60 = \$120$ – ie to cancel out the incorrect credit entry in the cash book and then to make the correct debit entry. However, the bank does not record the transfer until 5 July and so it will not appear in the bank statement.

2 Item (h). Two cheques have been paid to Jones, but one is now cancelled. Since the cash book is credited whenever a cheque is paid, it should be debited whenever a cheque is cancelled. The amount of unpresented cheques is reduced by the amount of the cancelled cheque.

BPP LEARNING MEDIA

BPP LEARNING MEDIA

BPP LEARNING MEDIA

BPP LEARNING MEDIA

Part B Accounting sys

Part B Accounting systems and accounts preparation | 13: Bank reconciliations   209

(b) BANK RECONCILIATION STATEMENT AT 30 JUNE 20X0

Balance per bank statement
Add: outstanding lodgements
(ie cheques paid in but not yet credited)
deposit interest not yet credited (note 1)

Less: unpresented cheques
less cheque to Jones cancelled (note 2)

Balance per corrected cash book

Assessment focus point

Notice that in preparing a bank reconciliation it is good practice to begi[n]
and end with the balance shown by the cash book. It is this corrected [balance that appears in the]
statement of financial position as 'cash at bank'. Questions sometimes
always, read the question carefully.

Question

From the information given below relating to PWW you are required:

(a) To make such additional entries in the cash account of PWW a[s]
balance at 31 October 20X2.

(b) To prepare a statement reconciling the corrected cash account
31 October 20X2 on the bank statement.

CASH AT BANK ACCOUNT IN THE LED[GER]

20X2 October		$	20X2 October	
1	Balance b/f	274	1	W
8	Q Manufacturing	3,443	1	Pe
8	R Cement	1,146	8	W
11	S Limited	638	8	Pe
11	T & Sons	512	15	W
11	U & Co	4,174	15	P
15	V	1,426	22	A
15	W Electrical	887	22	B
22	X and Associates	1,202	22	C
26	Y	2,875	22	D
26	Z	982	22	F
29	ABC	1,003	22	G
29	DEE Corporation	722	22	V
29	GHI	2,461	22	P
31	Balance c/f	14	25	
			26	
			26	
			26	
			28	

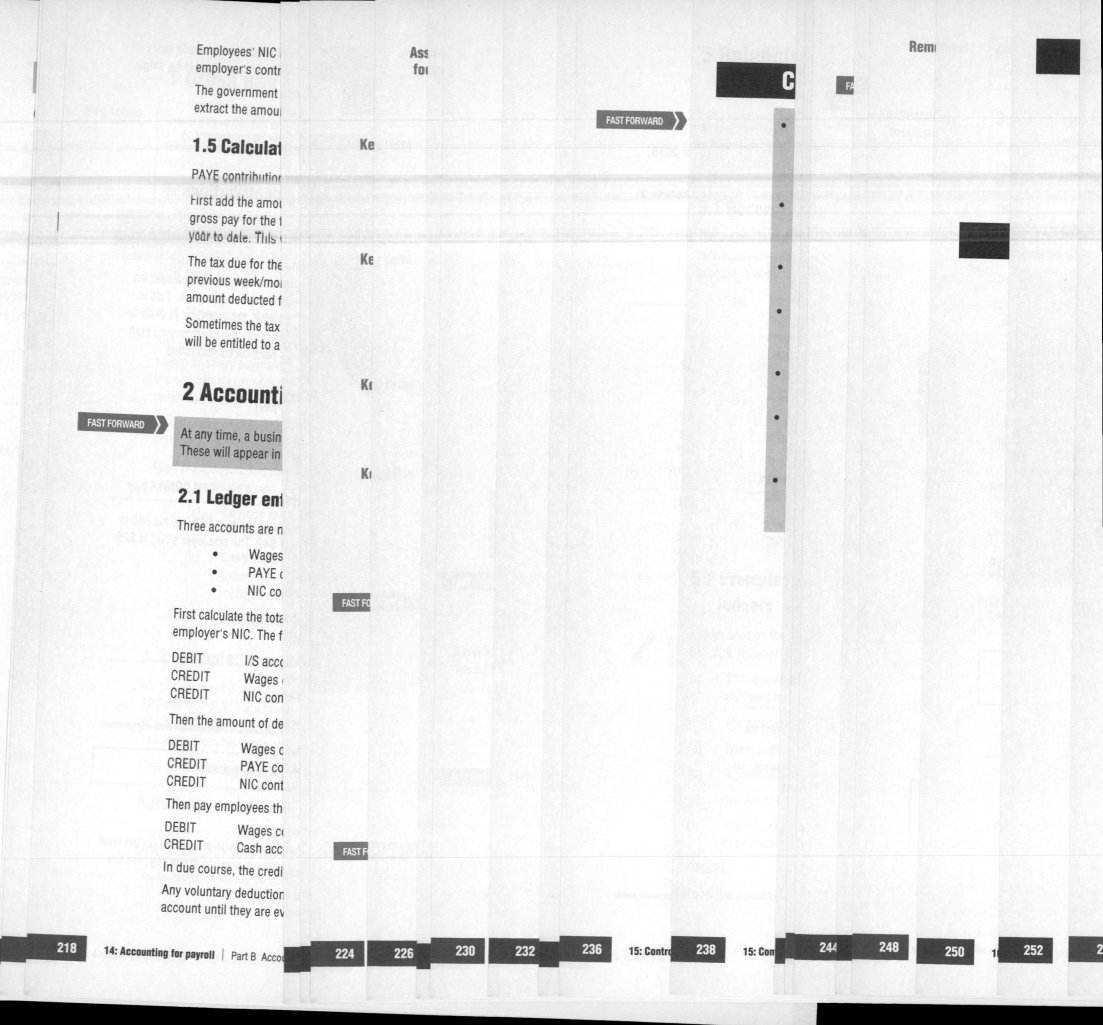

210   13: Bank reconciliations | Part B Accounting systems and accounts preparation
212   13: Bank re
218   14: Accounting for payroll | Part B Acco
224   226   230   232   236   15: Contro   238   15: Con   244   248   250   252

NEWBEGIN TOOLS
STATEMENT OF FINANCIAL POS

Non-current assets
Motor vehicles
Shop fittings

Current assets
Inventories
Receivables, less allowance for
Cash

Capital
Capital at 1 August 20X5
Net profit for the period

Less drawings
Capital at 31 January 20X6

Current liabilities
Trade payables

The bank overdraft has now been repai

1.2 Example: accounts pre

The following trial balance was extract
his financial year.

(i)   Stationery, postage and wrappi
(ii)   Telephone charges
(iii)   Electricity
(iv)   Cleaning and refreshments

(g)   Cash drawings by the proprietor, Alf N

(h)   The outstanding overdraft balance as a
        overdraft amounted to $40.

Prepare the income statement of Newbegin To
position as at that date. Ignore depreciation.

Answer

INCOME STATEMENT
FOR THE SIX MONTHS ENDED 31 JANUARY 2

Sales
        Opening inventories
        Purchases (note (a))

        Less closing inventories
Cost of goods sold
Gross profit
Discounts received (note (b))

Elcctricity (note (c))
Stationery, postage and wrapping
Bad debts written off
Allowance for receivables (note (d))
Telephone charges
Cleaning and refreshments
Interest and bank charges

Net profit

Notes

(a)   Purchases at cost $10,000 less 2% trad

(b)   5% of $8,000 = $400.

(c)   Expenses are grouped into sales and dis
        postage, bad debts and allowance for re
        charges and cleaning) and finance charg

(d)   2% of $3,000 = $60.

The preparation of a statement of financial posi
cash in hand.

Preparation of sole traders' accounts

17

Introduction

We have now reached our goal of preparing of the final accounts of a sole trader!

We will deal with the case of a trial balance and then making adjustments to produce final accounts.

This chapter also acts as a review of what we have covered to date.

Topic list	Syllabus references
1 Preparation of final accounts	C (1)

1 Preparation of final a

You should now be able to prepare a set o
end adjustments for depreciation, inventor

1.1 Adjustments to accounts

This chapter acts as a consolidation of all t

You should now use what you have learne
income statement and statement of financi

Question

The financial affairs of Newbegin Tools pri

NEWBEGIN TOOLS
STATEMENT OF FINANCIAL POSITION AS

Non-current assets
Motor vehicle
Shop fittings

Current assets
Inventories
Cash

Capital
Current liabilities
Bank overdraft
Trade payables

At the end of six months the business had

(a)   Goods were purchased on credit at

(b)   Trade discount received was 2% on
      debts to suppliers of $8,000. These

(c)   Closing inventories of goods were v

(d)   All sales were on credit and amount

(e)   Outstanding receivables balances at
      An allowance for receivables is to be

(f)   Cash payments were made in respec

(a)   Payables as at 31 January 20X

      The amount owing to payables
      purchases during the period (

      Payables as at 1 August 20X5
      Add purchases during the per

      Less settlement discounts rec

      Less payments to payables d

      * $8,000 less cash discount

(b)   Cash at bank and in hand at 3

      You need to identify cash pay

      (i)   *Cash received from s*
            Total sales in the peri
            Add receivables as at

            Less unpaid debts as
            Cash received

      (ii) *Cash paid*
            Trade payables (see
            Stationery, postage
            Telephone charges
            Electricity
            Cleaning and refres
            Bank charges and i
            Bank overdraft repa
            Drawings by propr

      Note. It is easy to forget so

      (iii) Cash in hand at 1 A
            Cash received in th

            Cash paid in the pe
            Cash at bank and i

(c)   When bad debts are writte
      Receivables in the stateme
      for receivables of $60 – ie

(d)   Non-current assets should

STEPHEN CHEE
TRIAL BALANCE AS AT 31 MAY 20X1

	Dr $	Cr $
Property, at cost	120,000	
Equipment, at cost	80,000	
Provisions for depreciation (as at 1 June 20X0)		
– on property		20,000
– on equipment		38,000
Purchases	250,000	
Sales		402,200
Stock, as at 1 June 20X0	60,000	
Discounts allowed	18,000	
Discounts received		4,800
Returns out		15,000
Wages and salaries	58,800	
Bad debts	4,600	
Loan interest	5,100	
Other operating expenses	17,700	
Trade payables		36,000
Trade receivables	38,000	
Cash in hand	300	
Bank	1,300	
Drawings	24,000	
Allowance for receivables		500
17% long term loan		30,000
Capital, as at 1 June 20X0		121,300
	667,800	667,800

The following additional information as at 31 May 20X1 is available.

(a)   Inventory as at the close of business has been valued at cost at $42,000.

(b)   Wages and salaries need to be accrued by $800.

(c)   Other operating expenses are prepaid by $300.

(d)   The allowance for receivables is to be adjusted so that it is 2% of trade receivables.

(e)   Depreciation for the year ended 31 May 20X1 has still to be provided for as follows.

      Property: 1.5% per annum using the straight line method; and
      Equipment: 25% per annum using the reducing balance method.

Required

Prepare Stephen Chee's income statement for the year ended 31 May 20X1 and his statement of financial position as at that date.

Solution

STEPHEN CHEE
INCOME STATEMENT
FOR THE YEAR ENDED 31 MAY 20X1

	$	$
Sales		402,200
Cost of sales		
Opening inventory	50,000	
Purchases	250,000	
Purchases returns	(15,000)	
	285,000	
Closing inventory	42,000	
		243,000
Gross profit		159,200
Other income – discounts received		4,800
		164,000
Expenses		
Operating expenses		
Wages and salaries ($58,800 + $800)	59,600	
Discounts allowed	18,000	
Bad debts (W1)	4,860	
Loan interest	5,100	
Depreciation (W2)	12,300	
Other operating expenses ($17,700 – $300)	17,400	
		117,260
Net profit for the year		46,740

STEPHEN CHEE

STATEMENT OF FINANCIAL POSITION AS AT 31 MAY 20X0

	Cost $	Accumulated depn. $	Net book value $
Non-current assets			
Property	120,000	21,800	98,200
Equipment	80,000	48,500	31,500
	200,000	70,300	129,700
Current assets			
Stock		42,000	
Trade receivables net of allowance for receivables ($38,000 – 760 (W1))		37,240	
Prepayments		300	
Bank		1,300	
Cash in hand		300	
			81,140
			210,840

	$	$
Capital		
Balance at 1 June 20X0		121,300
Net profit for the year		46,740
		168,040
Drawings		24,000
		144,040
Non-current liabilities		
17% loan		30,000
Current liabilities		
Trade payables	36,000	
Accruals	800	
		36,800
		210,840

Workings

		$
1	*Bad debts*	
	Previous allowance	500
	New allowance (2% × 38,000)	760
	Increase	260
	Per trial balance	4,600
	Income statement	4,860
2	*Depreciation*	
	Property	
	Opening provision	20,000
	Provision for the year (1.5% × 120,000)	1,800
	Closing provision	21,800
	Equipment	
	Opening provision	38,000
	Provision for the year (25% × 42,000)	10,500
	Closing provision	48,500
	Total charge in I/S	12,300

Donald Brown, a sole trader, extracted the following trial balance on 31 December 20X0.

TRIAL BALANCE AS AT 31 DECEMBER 20X0

	Debit $	Credit $
Capital at 1 January 20X0		26,094
Receivables	42,737	
Cash in hand	1,411	
Payables		35,404
Fixtures and fittings at cost	42,200	
Discounts allowed	1,304	
Discounts received		1,175
Inventory at 1 January 20X0	18,460	
Sales		491,620
Purchases	387,936	
Motor vehicles at cost	45,730	
Lighting and heating	6,184	
Motor expenses	2,862	
Rent	8,841	
General expenses	7,413	
Bank overdraft		19,861
Provision for depreciation		
Fixtures and fittings		2,200
Motor vehicles		15,292
Drawings	26,568	
	591,646	591,646

The following information as at 31 December is also available.

(a) $218 is owing for motor expenses.

(b) $680 has been prepaid for rent.

(c) Depreciation is to be provided of the year as follows.

Motor vehicles: 20% on cost
Fixtures and fittings: 10% reducing balance method

(d) Inventory at the close of business was valued at $19,926.

Required

Prepare Donald Brown's income statement for the year ended 31 December 20X0 and his statement of financial position at that date.

Tutorial note. You should note these points.

(a)   Discounts allowed are an expense of the business and should be shown as a deduction from gross profit. Similarly, discounts received is a revenue item and should be added to gross profit.

(b)   The figure for depreciation in the trial balance represents accumulated depreciation up to and including 20W9. You have to calculate the charge for the year 20X0 for the income statement and add this to the trial balance figure to arrive at the accumulated depreciation figure to be included in the statement of financial position.

DONALD BROWN
INCOME STATEMENT
FOR THE YEAR ENDED 31 DECEMBER 20X0

	$	$
Sales		491,620
Less cost of sales		
Opening inventory	18,460	
Purchases	387,936	
	406,396	
Closing inventory	19,926	
		386,470
Gross profit		105,150
Discounts received		1,175
		106,325
Less expenses:		
discounts allowed	1,304	
lighting and heating	6,184	
motor expenses (2,862 + 218)	3,080	
rent (8,841 – 680)	8,161	
general expenses	7,413	
depreciation (W)	13,146	
		39,288
Net profit		67,037

Working: depreciation charge

Motor vehicles: $45,730 \times 20\% = \$9,146$
Fixtures and fittings: $10\% \times \$(42,200 - 2,200) = \$4,000$
Total: $\$4,000 + \$9,146 = \$13,146$.

DONALD BROWN
STATEMENT OF FINANCIAL POSITION AS AT 31 DECEMBER 20X0

	Cost $	Depreciation $	Net $
Non-current assets			
Fixtures and fittings	42,200	6,200	36,000
Motor vehicles	45,730	24,438	21,292
	87,930	30,638	57,292
Current assets			
Inventory		19,926	
Receivables		42,737	
Prepayments		680	
Cash in hand		1,411	
			64,754
			122,046
Capital			
Balance b/f			26,094
Net profit for year			67,037
			93,131
Less drawings			26,568
			66,563
Current liabilities			
Payables		35,404	
Accruals		218	
Bank overdraft		19,861	
			55,483
			122,046

Chapter roundup

- You should now be able to prepare a set of final accounts for a sole trader from a trial balance after incorporating period end adjustments for depreciation, inventory, prepayments, accruals, bad debts, and allowances for receivables.

Quick quiz

1   Which of the following is the correct formula for cost of sales?

   A   Opening inventory – purchases + closing inventory.
   B   Purchases – closing inventory + sales.
   C   Opening inventory – closing inventory + purchases.
   D   Opening inventory + closing inventory – purchases.

2   The trial balance is the final phase prior to preparation of the accounts. True or false?

3   Which is the correct order of current assets in the statement of financial position?

   A   Bank, prepayments, receivables, inventory
   B   Inventory, receivables, prepayments, bank
   C   Inventory, prepayments, receivables, bank
   D   Inventory, bank, receivables, prepayments

Answers to quick quiz

1   C   Correct, this is a version of the more normal formula: opening inventory + purchases – closing inventory.
   A   Incorrect.
   B   Incorrect. Sales should never form part of cost of sales.
   C   Incorrect.

2   False.   The trial balance checks that the double entry has been done correctly. After the trial balance has been struck, there are usually adjustments (eg for accruals, prepayments, depreciation) before the financial statements are prepared.

3   B   Remember that current assets are listed in order of increasing liquidity (inventory being the least easy to turn into cash).

Now try the questions below from the Question Bank

Question numbers
76–77

Limited liability companies

Introduction

In this chapter we study the accounts of **limited liability companies**. The accounting rules and conventions for recording the business transactions of limited liability companies and then preparing their final accounts, are much the same as for sole traders. For example, companies will have a cash book, sales day book, purchase day book, journal, sales ledger, purchase ledger and nominal ledger etc. They also prepare an income statement annually, and a statement of financial position at the end of the accounting year.

We shall see that, in the statement of financial position, the treatment of assets and liabilities is basically the same but the particular nature of limited liability companies calls for changes in the owners' equity section. Similarly, in the income statement, the principal differences are found in the statement of other comprehensive income. There is also a statement of changes in equity, which shows how the profit or loss for the period has been divided.

One important difference is the legal requirement that limited liability companies must publish their accounts. The relevant legislation specifies certain information which must be included in the published financial statements of a limited liability company.

It should be stressed that, while you do not have to learn the published accounts formats by heart at this stage, it is important for you to have an overall awareness of the form of company accounts. In Chapter 20 you will learn about interpretation of accounts and this will include items in company accounts formats.

Topic list	Syllabus references
1 Limited liability companies	C (1)
2 Share capital and reserves	C (1)
3 Bonus and rights issues	C (1)
4 The final accounts of limited liability companies	A (2), C (2)
5 Loan stock	C (2)
6 Statement of changes in equity	C (2)
7 Taxation	C (2)
8 The ledger accounts of limited liability companies	C (2)

1 Limited liability companies

Company accounts preparation in the UK is governed by the Companies Act.

Companies issue shares to shareholders who enjoy limited liability.

Key terms

There are two classes of limited liability company in the UK.

(a) **Private companies.** These have the word 'limited' at the end of their name. Being private, they cannot invite members of the public to invest in their equity (shares).

(b) **Public companies.** These are much fewer in number than private companies, but are generally much larger in size. They have the words 'public limited company' – shortened to PLC or plc (or the Welsh language equivalent) at the end of their name. Public limited companies can invite members of the general public to invest in their equity, and the 'shares' of these companies are traded on a Stock Exchange.

Assessment focus point

Under IFRS, public companies are usually 'Inc' and private companies 'Co'.

1.1 Limited liability

Key term

Limited liability companies offer **limited liability** to their owners. This means that the liability of an owner is limited to any amounts not yet paid up for shares bought from the company. So, unlike sole traders, the owners (shareholders) of a company do not have to use their own, private, finances to pay payables if there are insufficient funds in the business.

2 Share capital and reserves

2.1 Share capital

The proprietors' capital in a limited liability company consists of **share capital**. A company issues **shares**, which are paid for by investors, who then become shareholders of the company.

When a company is set up with a **share capital** of, say, $100,000, it may be decided to issue

- 100,000 shares of $1 each nominal value
- 200,000 shares of 50c each
- 400,000 shares of 25c each
- 250,000 shares of 40c each

$1, 50c, 25c or 40c is the nominal value of the share. The nominal value is not the same as the market value, which is the price someone is prepared to pay for the share.

Key term

The **authorised share capital** is the maximum amount of share capital that the company is empowered to issue. Issued share capital is the nominal amount of share capital that has been issued to shareholders. This cannot exceed the authorised share capital. **Called up share capital** is the total amount of issued share capital for which the shareholders are required to pay. **Paid up share capital** is the amount of share capital paid by the shareholders.

2.2 Dividends

Key terms

Profits paid out to shareholders are called **dividends**.

- An **interim** dividend is a dividend paid part-way through the year
- At the end of the year, the company might pay a further **final** dividend.

The **total dividend** for the year is the sum of the interim and final dividends. (Not all companies pay an interim dividend. Interim dividends are commonly paid by public limited companies.)

Usually, at the end of an accounting year, a company's directors will propose a final dividend payment, but this will not yet have been paid. This means that the final dividend will be shown as a note to the financial statements. It is not a liability until the dividend is approved at the AGM.

2.3 The terminology of dividend

The terminology of dividend payments can be confusing, since they may be expressed either in the form, as 'x cents per share' or as 'y per cent'. In the latter case, the meaning is always 'y per cent of the **nominal** value of the shares in issue'. For example, suppose a company's issued share capital consists of 100,000 50c ordinary shares. The company's statement of financial position would include the following.

Called up share capital: 100,000 50c ordinary shares $50,000

If the directors wish to pay a dividend of $5,000, they may propose any of the following.

- A dividend of 5c per share (100,000 × 5c = $5,000)
- A dividend of 10% (10% × $50,000 = $5,000)
- A dividend of 10c in the pound ($50,000 × 10c = $5,000)

Any profits not paid out as dividends are put in reserves (see below).

2.4 Ordinary shares and preference shares

The two types of shares most often encountered are preference shares and ordinary shares.

FAST FORWARD

Preference shares carry the right to a fixed dividend which is expressed as a percentage of their nominal value: eg a 6% $1 preference share carries a right to an annual dividend of 6c.

Preference dividends have priority over ordinary dividends. If the directors of a company wish to pay a dividend (which they are not obliged to do) they must pay any preference dividend first. Otherwise, no ordinary dividend may be paid.

FAST FORWARD

Ordinary shares are by far the most common. They carry no right to a fixed dividend but are entitled to all profits left after payment of any preference dividend. In most companies only ordinary shares carry voting rights.

Should the company be wound up, any surplus is shared between the ordinary shareholders.

 Question

Dividends 1

At the year-end, the trial balance for KT shows a debit balance of $20,000 in respect of dividends. The Share Capital account of $1m comprises 200,000 5% preference shares of $1 with the balance made up of 50c ordinary shares. The dividends account represents a half-year's preference dividend and an interim ordinary dividend. A final dividend of 5c per ordinary share was proposed before the trial balance was prepared.

Calculate the interim and final dividends for each category of share.

Answer

A full year's dividend on the preference shares is 200,000 @ 5% = $10,000, therefore a half-year's dividend was $5,000, with a final dividend of the same amount.

The interim ordinary dividend was therefore $15,000 ($20,000 – $5,000).

As the share capital account amounts to $1m, $800,000 ($1m – $200k) must relate to ordinary shares. However, the ordinary shares are only 50c each, meaning that there are 1.6 million of them. The final dividend is therefore $80,000 (1.6m × 5c)

Assessment focus point

It is worth spending a few minutes getting to grips with dividend calculations, as they are a likely assessment topic. You are unlikely to get a calculation more difficult than that involved in the exercise above.

Question

Dividends 2

A company's share capital is:

50c	Ordinary shares	$2m
$1	6% preference shares	$1m

Dividends to ordinary shareholders have been:

		Amount	Date declared
20X2	Final dividend	4c per share	31 Jan 20X3
20X3	Interim dividend	3c per share	13 July 20X3
20X3	Final dividend	5c per share	20 Jan 20X4

What is the figure for dividends in the financial statements to 31 December 20X3?

A $160,000
B $220,000
C $320,000
D $340,000

Answer

D is correct.

	$
1m 6% preference shares	60,000
20X2 final (4c × 4m shares)	160,000
20X3 interim (3c × 4m shares)	120,000
Total	340,000

The 20X3 final dividend was declared after the year end and so will be disclosed in a note to the financial statements.

Solution

DEBIT   Cash
CREDIT   Ordinary share capital
CREDIT   Share premium account

A share premium account only comes into b
value. The market price of the shares, once
so if their market price goes up or down, th

2.8 Revaluation reserve

FAST FORWARD

A **revaluation reserve** is a statutory reserve

Revaluations frequently occur with freehold
show a more 'reasonable' value of the asset
impression about the financial position of th

When an asset is revalued the revaluation res
and its net book value before the revaluation

2.9 Example: revaluation rese

X Co bought freehold land and buildings for
buildings) is now $19,300. A professional va
the accounts. Show the entries to record thi

Solution

The revaluation surplus is $390,000 – $19,3

DEBIT   Freehold property
CREDIT   Revaluation reserve

The statement of financial position will then

Reserves
    Revaluation reserve
Non-current assets
    Freehold property (at valuation)

An unrealised capital profit (such as the $37(
(ie if the property is actually sold for $390,00

2.10 Distinction between reser

Key term

A **reserve** is an appropriation of distributable
amount charged against revenue as an expen

A provision relates either to a diminution in th
audit fees), the amount of which cannot be es
receivables etc) are dealt with in company ac

2.5 Reserves

FAST FORWARD

Reserves are profits that have not been distributed (paid out) to shareholders.

The ordinary shareholders' total investment in a company is called the **equity** and consists of ordinary share capital plus **reserves**.

Shareholders' funds is the total of all share capital, both ordinary and preference, and the reserves.

The important point to note is that all reserves are **owned** by the ordinary shareholders.

A distinction should be made between the two types of reserves.

Key terms

Statutory reserves are reserves which a company is required to set up by law and which are not available for the distribution of dividends.

Non-statutory reserves are reserves consisting of profits which are distributable as dividends, if the company so wishes.

2.5.1 Retained earnings

Key term

These are profits earned by the company and **not appropriated** by dividends, taxation or transfer to another reserve account. This reserve generally increases from year to year, as most companies do not distribute all their profits as dividends. If a loss is made in one particular year, a dividend can still be paid from previous years' retained earnings.

For example, if a company makes a loss of $100,000 in one year, yet has unappropriated profits from previous years totalling $250,000, it can pay a dividend not exceeding $150,000.

Very occasionally, you come across a debit balance on the retained earnings account. This indicates that the company has accumulated losses.

This is the most significant non-statutory reserve, and it is described in many different ways.

- Revenue reserve
- Retained profits
- Retained earnings
- Undistributed profits
- Unappropriated profits

Under IAS 1 (revised), it is called **retained earnings**.

2.5.2 Other non-statutory reserves

The company directors may choose to set up other reserves. These may have a specific purpose (for example plant and machinery replacement reserve) or not (for example general reserve). The creation of these reserves usually indicates a general intention not to distribute the profits involved at any future date, although legally any such reserves, being non-statutory, remain available for the payment of dividends.

Profits are transferred to these reserves by making an appropriation out of profits, usually profits for the year. Typically, you might come across the following.

Profit after taxation
Appropriations of profit
Dividend
Transfer to general reserve

Retained profits for the year
Retained profits b/f
Retained profits c/f

There is no real significance about the c_____
between the following two statement of _____

(a) Total assets
     Financed by
     Share capital
     Reserves: general (distributable_____
                retained earnings (di_____

(b) Total assets
     Financed by
     Share capital
     Reserves: retained earnings (distr_____

The establishment of a 'plant and machin_____
company to keep funds in the business t_____
represent distributable profits. The existe_____
non-current assets in the future, than the_____

Under IAS 1 (revised), all reserves are ad_____
financial position. The detail of movemen_____

2.6 The share premium acco_____

FAST FORWARD

The **share premium account** is a statutor_____
excess received over nominal value is cre_____

When a company is first incorporated (se_____
value and so there would be no share pre_____
not the nominal value. The price of any ne_____
between cash received by the company a_____
premium account.

2.7 Example

X Co issues 1,000 $1 ordinary shares at $_____

Question

(a) A public company has 10,000,000 25c shares in issue and their current value on the stock market is $4.97 per share. What is the value of share capital in the company's nominal ledger?

(b) The retained profits of a limited liability company the same thing as the trading account of a sole trader. True or false?

(c) A freehold property is revalued from $100,000 to $500,000. What is the balance on the revaluation reserve after this revaluation?

Answer

(a) $2.5m.
(b) False. The reserve is for *retained* profits, not profits of the current year only.
(c) $320,000 (ie $500,000 – $180,000).

3 Bonus and rights issues

FAST FORWARD

A company may choose to expand its capital base by issuing further shares to existing shareholders. It can do this by means of a bonus issues or a rights issue.

3.1 Bonus issues

A company may wish to increase its share capital without needing to raise additional finance by issuing new shares. For example, a profitable company might expand from modest beginnings over a number of years. Its profitability would be reflected in large balances on its reserves, while its original share capital might look like that of a much smaller business.

It is open to such a company to **re-classify some of its reserves as share capital**. This is purely a paper exercise which **raises no funds**. Any reserve may be re-classified in this way, including a share premium account or other statutory reserve. Such a re-classification **increases the capital base** of the company and gives **creditors greater protection**.

3.2 Example: bonus issue

BUBBLES CO
STATEMENT OF FINANCIAL POSITION (EXTRACT)

	$'000	$'000
Equity		
Share capital		
$1 ordinary shares (fully paid)		1,000
Reserves		
Share premium	500	
Undistributed profit (retained earnings)	2,000	
		2,500
Shareholders' funds		3,500

Bubbles decided to make a '3 for 2' bonus issue (ie 3 new shares for every 2 already held). So shares with a nominal value of $1,500,000 need to be issued.

The double entry is

		$'000	$'000
DEBIT	Share premium	500	
	Retained earnings	1,000	
CREDIT	Ordinary share capital		1,500

After the issue the statement of financial position is as follows

	$'000
Share capital	
$1 ordinary shares (fully paid)	2,500
Reserves	
Retained earnings	1,000
Shareholders' funds	3,500

1,500,000 new ('bonus') shares are issued to existing shareholders, so that if Mr X previously held 20,000 shares he will now hold 50,000. The total value of his holding should theoretically remain the same however, since the net assets of the company remain unchanged and his share of those net assets remains at 2% (ie 50,000/2,500,000; previously 20,000/1,000,000).

3.3 Rights issues

A rights issue (unlike a bonus issue) is an issue of shares for cash. The 'rights' are offered to existing shareholders, who can sell them if they wish.

3.4 Example: rights issue

Bubbles Co (above) decides to make a rights issue, shortly after the bonus issue. The terms are '1 for 5 @ $1.20' (ie one new share for every five already held, at a price of $1.20). Assuming that all shareholders take up their rights (which they are not obliged to) the double entry is:

		$'000	$'000
DEBIT	Cash	600	
CREDIT	Ordinary share capital		500
	Share premium		100

Mr X who previously held 50,000 shares will now hold 60,000, and the value of his holding should increase (all other things being equal) because the net assets of the company will increase. The new statement of financial position will show:

	$'000	$'000
Share capital		
$1 ordinary shares		3,000
Reserves		
Share premium	100	
Retained earnings	1,000	
		1,100
Shareholders' funds		4,100

The increase in funds of $600,000 represents the cash raised from the issue of 500,000 new shares at a price of $1.20 each.

Rights issues are a popular way of **raising cash** by issuing shares and they are **cheap to administer**. In addition, **shareholders retain control** of the business as their holding is not diluted.

The disadvantages of a rights issue is that shareholders are **not obliged** to take up their rights and so the issue could fail to raise the money required. For this reason companies usually try to find a broker to 'underwrite' the issue, ie who will buy any rights not taken up by the shareholders.

4 The final accounts of limited liability companies

The preparation and publication of the final accounts of limited liability companies in the UK are governed by the CA 2006. This permits the use of financial statements under IAS 1.

4.1 IAS 1 (revised) format

At this stage in your studies, you do not have to learn the detailed regulations laid down by IAS 1 (revised). However, the general format of the statement of financial position and statement of comprehensive income a limited liability company is important.

ABC CO
STATEMENT OF FINANCIAL POSITION AS AT 31 DECEMBER 20X2

	20X2		20X1	
	$'000	$'000	$'000	$'000
Assets				
Non-current assets				
Property, plant and equipment	X		X	
Goodwill	X		X	
Other intangible assets	X		X	
		X		X
Current assets				
Inventories	X		X	
Trade and other receivables	X		X	
Other current assets	X		X	
Cash and cash equivalents	X		X	
		X		X
Total assets		X		X
Equity and liabilities				
Equity				
Share capital	X		X	
Retained earnings	X		X	
Other components of equity	X		X	
		X		X
Non-current liabilities				
Long-term borrowings	X		X	
Long-term provisions	X		X	
		X		X
Current liabilities				
Trade and other payables	X		X	
Short-term borrowings	X		X	
Current portion of long-term borrowings	X		X	
Current tax payable	X		X	
		X		X
Total equity and liabilities		X		X

ABC CO
STATEMENT OF COMPREHENSIVE INCOME FOR THE YEAR ENDED 31 DECEMBER 20X2
Illustrating the classification of expenses by function

	20X2	20X1	
	$'000	$'000	
Revenue	X	X	
Cost of sales	(X)	(X)	
Gross profit	X	X	
Other income	X	X	
Distribution costs	(X)	(X)	
Administrative expenses	(X)	(X)	Income statement
Other expenses	(X)	(X)	
Finance costs	(X)	(X)	
Profit before tax	X	X	
Income tax expense	(X)	(X)	
Profit for the year	X	X	Statement of
Other comprehensive income:			other
Gains on property revaluation	X	X	comprehensive
Total comprehensive income for the year	X	X	income

Important!

Investments are non-current assets if the company intends to hold on to them for a long time, and current assets if they are only likely to be held for a short time before being sold.

Year end dividends proposed will not appear in the accounts unless they are proposed before the reporting date.

5 Loan stock

FAST FORWARD

If a company wants to raise funds without issuing shares, it can do so by means of a loan stock issue.

Key term

Loan stocks are long-term liabilities described on the statement of financial position as loan capital. They are different from share capital for the following reasons.

(a)   Shareholders are members of a company, while providers of loan capital are payables.

(b)   Shareholders receive dividends (appropriations of profit) whereas the holders of loan capital are entitled to a fixed rate of interest (an expense charged against revenue).

(c)   Loan capital holders can take legal action against a company if their interest is not paid when due, whereas shareholders cannot enforce the payment of dividends.

(d)   Loan stock are often secured on company assets, whereas shares are not.

5.1 Loan interest

Interest is calculated on the nominal value of loan capital, regardless of its market value. If a company has $700,000 (nominal value) 12% loan stock in issue, interest of $84,000 will be charged in the income statement per year. Interest is usually paid half-yearly and examination questions often require an accrual to be made for interest due at the year end. Accrued interest is shown as a current liability in the year-end statement of financial position.

For example, if a company has $700,000 of 12% loan stock in issue, pays interest on 30 June and 31 December each year, and ends its accounting year on 30 September, there would be an accrual of three months' unpaid interest (3/12 × $84,000) = $21,000 at the end of each accounting year that the debentures are still in issue.

6 Statement of changes in equity

6.1 Purpose of the statement

Essentially, profits are set aside (appropriated) for three purposes.

- Pay tax
- Pay dividends to shareholders (ordinary and preferred dividends)
- Reinvest in the business

The amount reinvested in the business is the amount left after the tax and dividends have been paid. This amount is called retained profit for the year.

The retained earnings at the beginning of the year is the reserve as described in paragraph 2.5.1. The retained earnings for the current year are added to this opening balance to give the retained earnings balance at the end of the year.

6.2 Statement of changes in equity (SOCIE)

ABC CO
STATEMENT OF CHANGES IN EQUITY

	Equity	Share premium a/c	Revaluation surplus	Other reserves	Retained earnings	Total
	$	$	$	$	$	$
Bal b/f	X	X	X	X	X	X
Issue of share capital	X	X				X
Dividends					(X)	(X)
Total comprehensive income for the year			X		X	X
Balance c/f	X	X	X	X	X	X

Further details are needed of any additions to reserves or utilisations of reserves during the period.

Note that the SOCIE only includes dividends **actually paid** during the year.

Assessment focus point

Statements of changes in equity are a very likely topic. Common errors include putting dividends in the main income statement and putting loan interest into the statement of changes in equity.

6.3 Example of published financial statements

The accountant of Wislon Co has prepared the following list of nominal ledger balances as at 31 December 20X7.

	$'000
50c ordinary shares (fully paid)	350
7% $1 preference shares (fully paid)	100
10% loans (secured)	200
Retained earnings 1 January 20X7	242
General reserve 1 January 20X7	171
Freehold land and buildings 1 January 20X7 (cost)	430
Plant and machinery 1 January 20X7 (cost)	830
Provision for depreciation	
Freehold buildings 1 January 20X7	20
Plant and machinery 1 January 20X7	222
Inventory 1 January 20X7	190
Sales	2,695
Purchases	2,152
Preference dividend	7
Ordinary dividend (interim)	8
Loan interest	10
Wages and salaries	254
Light and heat	31
Sundry expenses	113
Suspense account	135
Receivables	179
Payables	195
Cash	126

Notes

(a)   Sundry expenses include $9,000 paid in respect of insurance for the year ending 1 September 20X8. Light and heat does not include an invoice of $3,000 for electricity for the three months ending 2 January 20X8, which was paid in February 20X8. Light and heat also includes $20,000 relating to salesmen's commission.

(b)   The suspense account is in respect of the following items.

	$'000
Proceeds from the issue of 100,000 ordinary shares	120
Proceeds from the sale of plant	300
	420
Less paid to acquire Mary & Co	285
	135

(c)   The net assets of Mary & Co were purchased on 3 March 20X7. Assets were valued as follows.

	$'000
Investments	230
Inventory	34
	264

All the inventory acquired was sold during 20X7. The investments were still held by Wislon at 31 December 20X7.

(d)   The freehold property was acquired some years ago. The buildings element of the cost was estimated at $100,000 and the estimated useful life of the assets was fifty years. As at 31 December 20X7 the property is to be revalued at $800,000.

(e)   The plant which was sold had cost $350,000 and had a net book value of $274,000 as on 1 January 20X7. $36,000 depreciation is to be charged on plant and machinery for 20X7.

(f)   The loans have been in issue for some years. The 50c ordinary shares all rank for dividends at the end of the year.

(g)   The directors wish to provide for

       (i)   loan interest due
       (ii)   a transfer to general reserve of $16,000
       (iii)   audit fees of $4,000

(h)   Inventory as at 31 December 20X7 was valued at $220,000 (cost).

(i)   Taxation is to be ignored.

Required

Prepare the final accounts of Wislon Co.

Approach and suggested solution

(a)   The usual adjustments are needed for accruals and prepayments (insurance, light and heat, debenture interest and audit fees). The loan interest accrued is calculated as follows.

	$'000
Charge needed in I/S (10% × $200,000)	20
Amount paid so far, as shown in trial balance	10
Accrual – presumably six months' interest now payable	10

The accrued expenses shown in the statement of financial position comprise

	$'000
Loan interest	10
Light and heat	3
Audit fee	4
	17

(b)   The misposting of $20,000 to light and heat is also adjusted, by reducing the light and heat expense, but charging $20,000 to salesmen's commission.

(c)   Depreciation on the freehold building is calculated as $\frac{\$100,000}{50} = \$2,000$.

The net book value of the freehold property is then $430,000 – $20,000 – $2,000 = $408,000 at the end of the year. When the property is revalued a reserve of $800,000 – $408,000 = $392,000 is then created.

(d)   The profit on disposal of plant is calculated as proceeds $300,000 (per suspense account) less NBV $274,000 ie $26,000. The cost of the remaining plant is calculated at $830,000 – $350,000 = $480,000. The depreciation provision at the year end is made up of the following.

	$'000
Balance 1 January 20X7	222
Charge for 20X7	36
Less depreciation on disposals (350 – 274)	(76)
	182

(e) Goodwill arising on the purchase of Mary & Co is calculated as follows.

	$'000
Paid (per suspense account)	285
Assets at valuation	264
Goodwill	21

In the absence of other instructions, this is shown as an asset on the statement of financial position. The investments, being owned by Wislon at the year end, are also shown on the statement of financial position, whereas Mary's inventory, acquired and then sold, is added to the purchases figure for the year.

(f) The other item in the suspense account is dealt with as follows.

	$'000
Proceeds of issue of 100,000 ordinary shares	120
Less nominal value 100,000 × 50c	50
Excess of consideration over nominal value (= share premium)	70

(g) The transfer to general reserve increases that reserve to $171,000 + $16,000 = $187,000.

WISLON CO
STATEMENT OF COMPREHENSIVE INCOME FOR THE YEAR ENDING 31 DECEMBER 20X7

	$'000	$'000	$'000
Sales			2,695
Less cost of sales			
Opening inventory		190	
Purchases (2,152 + 34)		2,186	
		2,376	
Less closing inventory		220	
			2,156
Gross profit			539
Profit on disposal of plant			26
			565
Less expenses			
Wages, salaries and commission (254 + 20)		274	
Sundry expenses [113 − (2/3 × 9)]		107	
Light and heat (31 + 3 − 20)		14	
Depreciation: freehold buildings		2	
plant		36	
Audit fees		4	
Loan interest		20	
			457
Profit for the year			108
Other comprehensive income			
Gains on property revaluation			392
Total comprehensive income for the year			500

WISLON CO
STATEMENT OF CHANGES IN EQUITY FOR THE YEAR ENDING 31 DECEMBER 20X7

	Equity	Share premium	Revaluation reserve	General reserve	Retained earnings	Total
	$'000	$'000	$'000	$'000	$'000	$'000
Bal b/f	350	–	–	171	242	763
Share issue	50	70	–	–	–	120
Dividend payments	–	–	–	–	(15)	(15)
Total comprehensive income for the year	–	–	392	–	108	500
Transfer to general reserve	–	–	–	16	(16)	–
	400	70	392	187	319	1,368

WISLON LIMITED
STATEMENT OF FINANCIAL POSITION AS AT 31 DECEMBER 20X7

	Cost/ val'n $'000	Dep'n $'000	$'000
Non-current assets			
Property, plant and equipment			
Freehold property	800	–	800
Plant and machinery	480	182	298
	1,280	182	1,098
Goodwill			21
Investments			230
			1,349
Current assets			
Inventory		220	
Receivables		179	
Prepayment		6	
Cash		126	
			531
Total assets			1,880
Equity and liabilities			
Equity			
Called up share capital			
50c ordinary shares (350 + 50)		400	
7% $1 preference shares		100	
			500
Reserves			
Retained earnings		319	
Share premium		70	
Revaluation reserve		392	
General reserve		187	
			968
			1,468
Non-current liabilities			
10% loan stock (secured)			200
Current liabilities			
Payables		195	
Accrual expenses		17	
			212
			1,880

Notice that the question asked for final accounts, but did not specify in published format. Therefore these accounts show information that would appear in the notes in published format.

7 Taxation

7.1 Corporation tax

Companies pay **corporation tax** on the profits they earn. The charge for corporation tax on profits for the year is shown as a deduction from net profit before appropriations. In the statement of financial position, tax payable to the government is generally shown as a current liability (ie it has not yet been paid out at the year end).

When corporation tax on profits is calculated for the income statement the calculation is only an estimate of what the company thinks its tax liability will be. In subsequent dealings with the tax authorities, a different corporation tax charge might eventually be agreed. Any difference is adjusted in the estimated taxation charge for the following year.

7.2 Example: taxation

Urals Co made a profit before tax of $150,000 in the year to 30 September 20X3 and of $180,000 in the following year (to 30 September 20X4).

The estimated corporation tax for the first year was $60,000 and in the second year was $75,000. The actual tax charge in the year to 30 September 20X3 was finally agreed with HMRC at $55,000.

Required

Compute the charge for taxation in the year to 30 September 20X4.

Solution

	To 30 September	
	20X3	20X4
	$	$
Estimate of tax on profits	60,000	75,000
Actual tax charge	55,000	
Overestimate of tax in 20X3	5,000	
		(5,000)
Tax charge in year to 30 September 20X4		70,000

The effect will be to increase profits in 20X4 by $5,000, to correct the 'error' in 20X3 when profits were reduced by $5,000 due to the overestimate of the tax charge.

8 The ledger accounts of limited liability companies

8.1 Additional accounts

Limited liability companies keep ledger accounts and the only difference from the ledger accounts of sole traders is that some additional accounts need to be kept.

There will be an account for each of the following items.

    (a)   Taxation

            (i)   Tax charged against profits will be accounted for as follows.

DEBIT	I/S account
CREDIT	Taxation account

            (ii)   The outstanding balance on the taxation account will be a liability in the statement of financial position, until eventually paid, when the accounting entry would be as follows.

DEBIT	Taxation account
CREDIT	Cash

    (b)   *Dividends*

        A separate account will be kept for the dividends for each different class of shares (eg preference, ordinary).

        When dividends are paid the following entries would be made.

DEBIT	Dividends paid account
CREDIT	Cash

    (c)   *Loan stocks*

        Loan stocks are a long term liability and will be shown as a credit balance in a loan stock account. Interest payable on such loans is not credited to the loan account, but is credited to a separate payables account for interest until it is eventually paid.

DEBIT	Interest account (an expense, chargeable against profits)
CREDIT	Interest payable (a current liability until eventually paid).

    (d)   *Share capital and reserves*

        There will be a separate account for each different class of share capital and for each different type of reserve. The balance on the share capital account will always be a credit and the balance on the reserve account will nearly always be a credit.

Chapter roundup

- Company accounts preparation in the UK is governed by the Companies Act.

- Companies issue shares to shareholders who enjoy limited liability.

- The proprietors' capital in a limited liability company consists of **share capital**. A company issues **shares**, which are paid for by investors, who then become shareholders of the company.

- **Preference shares** carry the right to a fixed dividend which is expressed as a percentage of their nominal value: eg a 6% $1 preference share carries a right to an annual dividend of 6c.

- **Ordinary shares** are by far the most common. They carry no right to a fixed dividend but are entitled to all profits left after payment of any preference dividend. In most companies only ordinary shares carry voting rights.

- **Reserves** are profits that have not been distributed (paid out) to shareholders.

- The ordinary shareholders' total investment in a company is called the **equity** and consists of ordinary share capital plus **reserves**.

- **Shareholders' funds** is the total of all share capital, both ordinary and preference, and the reserves.

- The important point to note is that all reserves are **owned** by the ordinary shareholders.

- The **share premium account** is a statutory reserve created if shares are issued for more than their nominal value. The excess received over nominal value is credited to the share premium account.

- A **revaluation reserve** is a statutory reserve which must be created when a company revalues its non-current assets.

- A company may choose to expand its capital base by issuing further shares to existing shareholders. It can do this by means of a bonus issues or a rights issue.

- The preparation and publication of the final accounts of limited liability companies in the UK are governed by the CA 2006. This permits the use of financial statements under IAS 1.

- If a company wants to raise funds without issuing shares, it can do so by means of a loan stock issue.

1   The nominal value of a share is?

    A   Its market price
    B   The price at which it was issued
    C   The price which it can be purchased for
    D   The 'face value' of a share

2   What does the phrase 'called up share capital' mean?

    A   The total amount of issued share capital which the shareholders are required to pay for
    B   The share capital actually issued
    C   The amount of share capital paid by the shareholders
    D   The amount of capital which is company has decided to issue

3   A provision is an amount charged as an expense, while a reserve is an appropriation of profit for a specific purpose. True or false?

4   At the year end a proposed dividend may be declared. Which of the following statements is correct regarding the proposed dividend?

    A   Treated as an expense in the I/S account
    B   Shown in the statement of financial position as a long term liability
    C   If declared after the reporting date, it is merely disclosed by note
    D   It is always the total profit which the company has agreed to distribute for the year

Answers to quick quiz

1   D   This is correct, the nominal value can be any value.
    A   Incorrect, the quoted price bears no relationship to the nominal value.
    B   This will be nominal value plus a premium on issue which in total equals the issue price.
    C   This is the market price.

2   A   Correct. Called up share capital means the capital which has been paid for plus current 'calls' outstanding.

    B   This is issued capital.

    C   This is paid up capital.

    D   This capital has not yet been issued and must be less than authorised capital.

3   True. A provision is an amount charged as an expense, while a reserve is an appropriation of profit for a specific purpose.

4   C   Correct.

    A   Dividends are appropriations of profit not expenses and are shown in the SOCIE.

    B   Proposed dividends are current liabilities, but only if declared before the reporting date.

    D   There may be an interim dividend as well, so the total distribution equals interim dividend paid plus proposed final dividend.

Now try the questions below from the Question Bank

Question numbers
78–81

Incomplete records

Introduction

So far in your work on preparing the final accounts for a sole trader we have assumed that a full set of records is kept. In practice many sole traders do not keep a full set of records and you must apply certain techniques to arrive at the necessary figures.

Incomplete records questions are a very good test of your understanding of the way in which a set of accounts is built up.

Limited liability companies are obliged by law to keep proper accounting records. However a small company may still lose records eg in a fire.

Topic list	Syllabus references
1 Incomplete records questions	C (1)
2 The opening statement of financial position	C (1)
3 Credit sales and receivables	C (1)
4 Purchases and trade payables	C (1)
5 Establishing purchases, inventories, or cost of sales	C (1)
6 Using gross profit margin and mark-up to find figures in the trading account	C (1)
7 Stolen goods or goods destroyed	C (1)
8 The cash book	C (1)
9 Accruals and prepayments	C (1)
10 Drawings	C (1)
11 The business equation	C (1)
12 Dealing with incomplete records problems	C (1)
13 Using a receivables account to calculate both cash sales and credit sales	C (1)

1 Incomplete records questions

Incomplete records occur when a business does not have a full set of accounting records because:

(a)   The proprietor of the business does not keep a full set of accounts.

(b)   Some of the business accounts are accidentally lost or destroyed.

1.1 Preparing accounts from incomplete records

The accountant must prepare a set of year-end accounts for the business ie an income statement, and a statement of financial position. Since the business does not have a full set of accounts, it is not a simple matter of closing off accounts and transferring balances to the income statement, or showing outstanding balances in the statement of financial position. The task of preparing the final accounts involves establishing the following.

- Cost of purchases and other expenses
- Total amount of sales
- Amount of payables, accruals, receivables and prepayments at the end of the year

Key term

> The final accounts you are asked to prepare a may include a **statement of affairs**. This simply means a statement of financial position in summary form because there is insufficient data for a full one, or one which is not in a standard format.

To understand what incomplete records are about, it will obviously be useful now to look at what exactly might be incomplete. The items we shall consider in turn are:

(a)   The opening statement of financial position.

(b)   Credit sales and receivables.

(c)   Purchases and trade payables.

(d)   Purchases, inventories and the cost of sales.

(e)   Stolen goods or goods destroyed.

(f)   The cash book.

(g)   Accruals and prepayments.

(h)   Drawings.

2 The opening statement of financial position

Where accounts for the previous period are not available, the accountant will have to reconstruct an opening statement of financial position.

2.1 Example: opening statement of financial position

A business has the following assets and liabilities as at 1 January 20X3.

	$
Fixtures and fittings at cost	7,000
Provision for depreciation, fixtures and fittings	4,000
Motor vehicles at cost	12,000
Provision for depreciation, motor vehicles	6,800
Inventory	4,500
Trade receivables	5,200
Cash at bank and in hand	1,230
Trade payables	3,700
Prepayment	450
Accrued rent	2,000

You are required to prepare a statement of financial position for the business, inserting a balancing figure for proprietor's capital.

Solution

STATEMENT OF FINANCIAL POSITION AS AT 1 JANUARY 20X3

	$	$
Non-current assets		
Fixtures and fittings at cost	7,000	
Less accumulated depreciation	4,000	
		3,000
Motor vehicles at cost	12,000	
Less accumulated depreciation	6,800	
		5,200
		8,200
Current assets		
Inventory	4,500	
Trade receivables	5,200	
Prepayment	450	
Cash	1,230	
		11,380
		19,580
Proprietor's capital as at 1 January 20X3 (balancing figure)		13,880
Current liabilities		
Trade payables	3,700	
Accrual	2,000	
		5,700
		19,580

3 Credit sales and receivables

FAST FORWARD

If a business does not keep a record of its sales on credit, the value of these sales can be derived from the opening balance of trade receivables, the closing balance of trade receivables, and the payments received from trade receivables during the period.

Formula to learn

	$
Credit sales are:	
Payments received from trade receivables	X
Plus closing balance of trade receivables (since these represent sales in the current period for which cash payment has not yet been received)	X
Less opening balance of trade receivables (these will represent sales made in a **previous** period)	(X)
	X

Throughout this chapter, we will give you a number of formulae to learn. You must learn these formats as they will not be given in the assessment.

3.1 Example: sales and receivables

A business had trade receivables of $1,750 on 1 April 20X4 and $3,140 on 31 March 20X5. If payments received from trade receivables during the year to 31 March 20X5 were $28,490, and there were no bad debts, calculate credit sales for the period.

Solution

	$
Cash received from receivables	28,490
Plus closing receivables	3,140
Less opening receivables	(1,750)
Credit sales	29,880

The same calculation could be made in a T account, with credit sales being the balancing figure to complete the account.

RECEIVABLES

	$		$
Opening balance b/f	1,750	Cash received	28,490
Credit sales (balancing fig)	29,880	Closing balance c/f	3,140
	31,630		31,630

The same interrelationship between balances can be used to derive a missing figure for cash from receivables (or opening or closing receivables), given the values for the three other items.

3.2 Example: to find cash received

Opening receivables are $6,700, closing receivables are $3,200 and credit sales for the period are $69,400. What was cash received from receivables during the period?

Solution

RECEIVABLES

	$		$
Opening balance	6,700	Cash received (balancing figure)	72,900
Sales (on credit)	69,400	Closing balance c/f	3,200
	76,100		76,100

If there are bad debts during the period, the value of sales will be increased by the amount of bad debts written off, no matter whether they relate to opening receivables or credit sales during the current period.

Question   Credit sales

Opening receivables are $1,500, closing receivables are $1,800. During the year $45,800 was received from receivables including $800 in respect of debts written off in an earlier period. $3,200 of debts were written off and the allowance for receivables increased by $700. What are the credit sales for the year?

$48,500.

RECEIVABLES ACCOUNT

	$		$
B/d	1,500	Cash	45,000
Credit sales (balance)	48,500	Bad debts expense	3,200
		C/d	1,800
	50,000		50,000

Remember that cash received from debts written off in an earlier period is not credited to receivables, and that the movement in the allowance for receivables does not go through receivables.

4 Purchases and trade payables

FAST FORWARD

A similar relationship exists between purchases of inventory during a period, the opening and closing balances for trade payables, and amounts paid to trade payables during the period.

Formula to learn

	$
Payments to trade payables during the period	X
Plus closing balance of trade payables (since these represent purchases in the current period for which payment has not yet been made)	X
Less opening balance of trade payables (these debts, paid in the current period, relate to purchases in a previous period)	(X)
Purchases during the period	X

4.1 Example: purchases and trade payables

A business had trade payables of $3,728 on 1 October 20X5 and $2,645 on 30 September 20X6. If payments to trade payables during the year to 30 September 20X6 were $31,479, what was purchases during the year?

Solution

	$
Payments to trade payables	31,479
Plus closing balance of trade payables	2,645
Less opening balance of trade payables	(3,728)
Purchases	30,396

The same calculation could be made in a T account, with purchases being the balancing figure to complete the account.

PAYABLES

	$		$
Cash payments	31,479	Opening balance b/f	3,728
Closing balance c/f	2,645	Purchases (balancing figure)	30,396
	34,124		34,124

5 Establishing purchases, inventories, or cost of sales

FAST FORWARD

In some questions you must use the information in the trading account rather than the trade payables account to find the cost of purchases. This information could also be used to find inventories or cost of sales.

Formula to learn

		$
Since	opening inventories	X
	plus purchases	X
	less closing inventories	(X)
	equals the cost of goods sold	X
then	the cost of goods sold	X
	plus closing inventories	X
	less opening inventories	(X)
	equals purchases	X

5.1 Example: using a trading account

The inventory of a business on 1 July 20X6 was $8,400, and an inventory count at 30 June 20X7 showed inventory to be valued at $9,350. Sales for the year to 30 June 20X7 are $80,000, and the cost of goods sold was $60,000. What were the purchases during the year?

Solution

	$
Cost of goods sold	60,000
Plus closing inventory	9,350
Less opening inventory	(8,400)
Purchases	60,950

6 Using gross profit margin and mark-up to find figures in the trading account

A question may ask you to use profit percentages to calculate sales or cost of sales.

FAST FORWARD

Where inventory, sales or purchases is the unknown figure, it will be necessary to use information on gross profit percentages in order to construct a trading account in which the unknown figure can be inserted as a balance.

Formula to learn

Gross margin is: $\dfrac{\text{Gross profit}}{\text{Sales}}$ Mark-up is: $\dfrac{\text{Gross profit}}{\text{Cost of goods sold}}$ (also described as gross profit on cost)

6.1 Example

Sales are $1,000 and cost of goods sold are $600. What are the profit margin and mark-up?

Left page

Required

(a)   Prepare a two column cash book for the period.

(b)   Prepare the income statement for the year to 31 December 20X7 and the sta[...] December 20X7.

Discussion and solution

A two column cash book is completed as follows.

(a)   Enter the opening cash balances.

(b)   Enter the information given about cash payments (and any cash receipts, if [...] in the problem).

(c)   The cash receipts banked are a 'contra' entry, being both a debit (bank colu[...] column) in the same account.

(d)   Enter the closing cash in hand (cash in the bank at the end of the period is [...]

CASH BOOK

	Cash in hand $	Bank $		Cash[...]
Balance b/f	200	3,000	Trade payables	
Cash receipts banked (contra)		41,750	Sundry expenses	
Sales*	40,000		Drawings	
			Cash receipts banked (contra)	
Balance c/f		*1,250	Balance c/f	
	48,200	46,000		

* Balancing figure

(e)   The closing balance of money in the bank is a balancing figure.

(f)   Since all sales are for cash, a balancing figure that can be entered in the cas[...] (debit) column.

It is important to notice that since not all receipts from cash sales are banked, the [...] is the balance on the cash account or it could be calculated as:

Receipts banked
Plus expenses and drawings paid out of the till in cash
$(800 + 1,500 + 3,700)
Plus any cash stolen (here there is none)
Plus the closing balance of cash in hand

Less the opening balance of cash in hand
Equals cash sales

The cash book has enabled us to establish both the closing balance for cash in the [...] sales. Now calculate purchases.

Middle page

(a)   The first 'unknown' is the am[...] account.

Payments to payables
Closing balance c/f

(b)   The cost of goods sold is als[...] for the period.

Sales   (10[...]
Gross profit   (33[...]
Cost of goods sold   (66[...]

(c)   The cost of the goods stolen[...]

Opening inventory at cost
Purchases

Less closing inventory (afte[...]
Cost of goods sold and goo[...]
Cost of goods sold (see (b)[...]
Cost of goods stolen

(d)   The cost of the goods stole[...] follows.

BEAU GULLARD
TRADING ACCOUNT FOR T[...]

Sales
Less cost of goods sold
    Opening inventory
    Purchases

        Less inventory stole[...]

Gross profit

8 The cash book

If no cash book has been kept it [...] column bank/cash book.

Right page

Solution

	$
Sales	1,000
Cost of goods sold	600
Gross profit	400

Profit margin is: $\dfrac{\$400}{\$1,000} = 40\%$ Mark-up is: $\dfrac{\$400}{\$600} = 66^2/_3\%$

Question

Purchases

At 1 May 20X3 inventory was $4,000, at 30 April 20X4 it was $3,000. Sales for the year were $80,000 and the business always has a mark up of 33⅓%. What were purchases for the year?

Answer

Working backwards:

	$	%
Purchases	59,000	
Opening inventory	4,000	
	63,000	
Less: Closing inventory	3,000	
Cost of sales	60,000	100
Gross profit or mark up	20,000	33⅓
Sales	80,000	133⅓

Take care that you correctly interpret whether you are dealing with gross profit on sales (margin) or gross profit on cost of sales (mark-up).

7 Stolen goods or goods destroyed

A similar type of calculation can derive the value of goods stolen or destroyed.

7.1 Example: cost of goods destroyed

Orlean Flames is a shop which sells fashion clothes. On 1 January 20X5, it had inventory which cost $7,345. During the 9 months to 30 September 20X5, the business purchased goods from suppliers costing $106,420. Sales during the same period were $154,000. The shop makes a gross profit of 40% on **cost** (mark-up) for everything it sells. On 30 September 20X5, there was a fire in the shop which destroyed most of the inventory in it. Only a small amount of inventory, known to have cost $350, was undamaged and still fit for sale.

How much inventory was lost in the fire?

Solution

(a)

	$
Sales (140%)	154,000
Gross profit (40%)	44,000
Cost of goods sold (100%)	110,000

Page 296 (left)

(b)

Opening inventory, at co
Plus purchases

Less closing inventory,
Equals cost of goods so

(c)

Cost of goods sold and
Cost of goods sold
Cost of goods lost

7.2 Accounting for inv

When inventory is stolen, destro

The account that is to be debite

(a) If the lost goods
statement.

DEBIT   I/S
CREDIT   Tr

(b) If the lost goods
cost of the lost g

DEBIT   In
CREDIT   Tr

with the cost of
account is then

DEBIT   Ca
CREDIT   In

Question

Beau Gullard runs a jewellery s
and his trade payables were $3

During the six months to 30 Ju
value (margin) of everything h

On 30 June, there was a burgl

In trying to establish how muc

(a) he knew from his bank
(b) he currently owed paya

Required

(a) Calculate the amount
(b) Prepare a trading acc

Page 298 (middle)

8.1 Writing up the cash book

We have already seen in this chapter that information about cash receipts or pay

- Purchases during a period
- Credit sales during a period

Other items of receipts or payments might be relevant to establishing

- Cash sales
- Certain expenses in the I/S account
- Drawings by the business proprietor

Often, to answer a question, we need to write up a cash book. Where there appea
payments in cash (ie notes and coins), then it is helpful to construct a two colum
one column for cash receipts and payments, and one column for money paid int

8.2 Example: two column cash book

Jonathan Slugg owns and runs a shop selling fishing tackle, making a gross pro
sells. He does not keep a cash book.

On 1 January 20X7 the statement of financial position of his business was as fo

Net non-current assets
Inventory
Cash in the bank
Cash in the till

Trade payables

Proprietor's capital

In the year to 31 December 20X7

(a) there were no sales on credit.

(b) $41,750 in receipts were banked.

(c) the bank statements of the period show the following payments.

		$
(i)	to trade payables	36,000
(ii)	sundry expenses	5,600
(iii)	in drawings	4,400

(d) payments were also made in cash out of the till.

		$
(i)	to trade payables	800
(ii)	sundry expenses	1,500
(iii)	in drawings	3,700

At 31 December 20X7, the business had cash in the till of $450 and trade payable
was not known and the value of closing inventory has not yet been calculated. Th
further non-current assets were purchased during the year. The depreciation cha

---

Page 300 (right)

	$		$
Cash book:		Balance b/f	1,200
Payments from bank	36,000	Purchases (balancing figure)	37,000
Cash book:			
Payments in cash	800		
Balance c/f	1,400		
	38,200		38,200

The gross profit margin of 25% on cost indicates that the cost of the goods sold is $38,400.

	$
Sales (125%)	48,000
Gross profit (25%)	9,600
Cost of goods sold (100%)	38,400

The closing inventory amount is now a balancing figure in the trading account.

JONATHAN SLUGG
INCOME STATEMENT
FOR THE YEAR ENDED 31 DECEMBER 20X7

	$	$
Sales		48,000
Less cost of goods sold		
Opening inventory	10,000	
Purchases	37,000	
	47,000	
Less closing inventory (balancing figure)	8,600	
		38,400
Gross profit (25/125 × $48,000)		9,600
Expenses		
Sundry $(1,500 + 5,600)	7,100	
Depreciation	900	
		8,000
Net profit		1,600

JONATHAN SLUGG
STATEMENT OF FINANCIAL POSITION AS AT 31 DECEMBER 20X7

	$	$
Net non-current assets $(20,000 – 900)		19,100
Inventory	8,600	
Cash in the till	450	
		9,050
		28,150

Proprietor's capital
Balance b/f ... 32,000
Net profit for the year ... 1,600
... 33,600
Drawings $(3,700 + 4,400) ... (8,100)
Balance c/f ... 25,500

Current liabilities
Bank overdraft ... 1,250
Trade payables ... 1,400
... 2,650
... 28,150

8.3 Theft of cash from the till

When cash is stolen from the till, the amount stolen will be a credit entry in the cash book, and a debit in either the I/S account or insurance claim account, depending on whether the business is insured.

9 Accruals and prepayments

9.1 Working out the charge

Where there is an accrued expense or a prepayment, the charge to be made in the I/S account for the item concerned should be found from the opening balance b/f, the closing balance c/f, and cash payments for the item during the period.

The charge in the I/S account is perhaps most easily found as the balancing figure in a T account.

9.2 Example: prepayments

On 1 April 20X6 a business had prepaid rent of $700. During the year to 31 March 20X7 it pays $9,300 in rent and at 31 March 20X7 the prepayment of rent is $1,000.

Calculate the I/S figure for rent expense.

Solution

The cost of rent in the I/S account for the year to 31 March 20X7 is the balancing figure in the following T account. (Remember that a prepayment is a current asset, and so is a debit balance b/f.)

RENT EXPENSE

	$		$
Prepayment: balance b/f	700	I/S (balancing figure)	9,000
Cash	9,300	Prepayment: balance c/f	1,000
	10,000		10,000
Balance b/f	1,000		

9.3 Example: Accrual

Similarly, if a business has accrued telephone expenses as at 1 July 20X6 of $850, pays $6,720 in telephone bills during the year to 30 June 20X7, and has accrued telephone expenses of $1,140 as at 30 June 20X7.

FAST FORWARD

1 Ra...

1.1 ...

When ...
finan...

If the ...
merely ...
need ...

2 P...

2.1 ...

Key term

Profit ...
is calc...

For ex...
This a...

2.2 Asset turnover

Key term

Asset ...

Net a...

For ex...

$720...
$360...

Cal...

So...

The ...
foll...

___

C
E...

1 Given cash s...
receivables (...

A $36,0...
B $38,0...
C $40,0...
D $25,0...

2 A business h...
payments to ...

A $27,5...
B $29,5...

3 The term 'inc...

A   The bu...
B   The re...
C   Small...
D   The bu...

4 A business ha...
van $5,000, i...
$1,200.

A $10,20...
B $9,800...

FAST FORWARD

Dra...
bus...

Assessment focus point

Dra...
rec...

(a)

(b)

10...

Wh...

10...

You...

2.4 Relationship between ratios

You may already have realised that there is a mathematical connection between return on capital employed, profit margin and asset turnover, since sales in the right-hand side of the equation below cancel out.

Formula to learn

$$\frac{Profit}{Capital\,employed} = \frac{Profit}{Sales} \times \frac{Sales}{Capital\,employed}$$

ROCE = Profit margin × Asset turnover

Assessment focus point

You **must** learn these formulae, as they will not be given in the assessment

This is important. If we accept that ROCE is the most important single measure of business performance, comparing profit with the amount of capital invested, we can go on to say that business performance is dependent on two separate 'subsidiary' factors, each of which contributes to ROCE.

(a) Profit margin.
(b) Asset turnover.

For this reason, just as ROCE is sometimes called the **primary ratio**, the profit margin and asset turnover ratios are sometimes called the **secondary ratios**.

The implications of this relationship must be understood. Suppose that a return on capital employed of 20% is thought to be a good level of business performance in the retail trade for electrical goods.

(a) Company A might decide to sell its products at a fairly high price and make a profit margin on sales of 10%. It would then need only an asset turnover of 2.0 times to achieve a ROCE of 20%:

20% = 10% × 2

(b) Company B might decide to cut its prices so that its profit margin is only 2½%. Provided that it can achieve an asset turnover of 8 times a year, attracting more customers with its lower prices, it will still make the desired ROCE:

20% = 2½% × 8

Company A might be a department store and company B a discount warehouse. Each will have a different selling price policy, but each, in its own way, can be effective in achieving a target ROCE. In this example, if we supposed that both companies had capital employed of $100,000 and a target return of 20% or $20,000.

(a) Company A would need annual sales of $200,000 to give a profit margin of 10% and an asset turnover of 2 times

$$\frac{\$20,000}{\$100,000} = \frac{\$20,000}{\$200,000} \times 2$$

(b) Company B would need annual sales of $800,000 to give a profit margin of only 2½% but an asset turnover of 8 times.

$$\frac{\$20,000}{\$100,000} = \frac{\$20,000}{\$800,000} \times 8$$

FAST FORWARD

The interpretation of financial statements requires a large measure of common sense.

It might sell all the inventories for
$3,500. The statement of financial

Inventories
Receivables
Cash

Payables
Working capital

(The increase in working capital t

The receivables for $4,500 will ev

Inventories
Receivables
Cash (2,000 + 4,500 – 3,500)

Payables
Working capital

However, if the inventories are so
the cycle of trading will continue a

Inventories
Receivables
Cash

Payables
Working capital (boosted by furth

From this basic example you mig
operations. Purchases add to inve
for their goods. The cycle of oper;

3.3 The operating cycl

The **operating cycle** (or cash cyc
sale of finished goods.

A firm buys raw materials, probal
issued to the production departm
warehouse for some time before
the raw materials purchased. If cu
eventually received

The cash cycle, or operating cycle
the time cash is received in from

This cycle of repeating events is s

Clearly, a higher return on capital employed can be obtained by increasing the profit margin or the asset turnover ratio. The profit margin can be increased by reducing costs or by raising selling prices.

However, if selling prices are raised, it is likely that sales demand will fall, with the possible consequence that the asset turnover will also decline. If higher prices mean lower sales turnover, the increase in profit margin might be offset by the fall in asset turnover, so that total return on capital employed might not improve.

2.5 Example: profit margin and asset turnover

Suppose that Swings and Roundabouts Ltd achieved the following results in 20X6.

Sales	$100,000
Profit	$5,000
Capital employed	$20,000

The company's management wish to decide whether to raise its selling prices. They think that if they do so, they can raise the profit margin to 10% and by introducing extra capital of $55,000, sales turnover would be $150,000.

Evaluate the decision in terms of the effect on ROCE, profit margin and asset turnover.

Solution

Currently the ratios are

Profit margin (5/100)	5%
Asset turnover (100/20)	5 times
ROCE (5/20)	25%

With the proposed changes, the profit would be 10% × $150,000 = $15,000, and the asset turnover would be:

$$\frac{\$150,000}{\$(20,000+55,000)} = 2 \text{ times, so that the ratios would be}$$

$$\text{Profit margin} \times \text{Asset turnover} = \text{ROCE}$$

$$0\% \times 2 \text{ times} = 20\% \left(\frac{\$15,000}{\$75,000}\right)$$

In spite of increasing the profit margin and raising the total volume of sales, the extra assets required ($55,000) only raise total profits by $(15,000 – 5,000) = $10,000.

The return on capital employed falls from 25% to 20% because of the sharp fall in asset turnover from 5 times to 2 times.

 Question   Ratios

A trader has the following results.

	$
Sales	200,000
Profit	36,000
Capital employed	120,000

Question

Using the information in the las...

Relevant figures as at 31 Decem...

10% loans
Ordinary share capital
Retained earnings

Answer

Average capital employed = (59...

$$ROCE = \frac{120,000}{595,000} = 20.2\%$$

3 Working capita

FAST FORWARD

Working capital is the differenc...
(such as trade payables and a b...

3.1 Current assets an

Current assets are items which...
sold to customers and create re...

Current liabilities are items whi...
overdraft is usually regarded as...
immediately).

In statements of financial posit...
cash (current assets) and amou...

3.2 Working capital a

Current assets and current liab...
buying and selling which is car...

Inventories
Receivables
Cash

Payables
Working capital

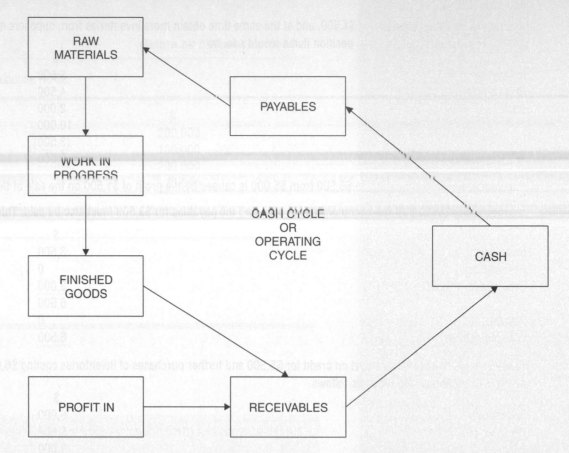

Suppose that a firm buys raw materials on 1½ months' credit, holds them in store for 1 month and then issues them to the production department. The production cycle is very short, but finished goods are held for 1 month before they are sold. Receivables take two months' credit. The cash cycle would be

	Months
Raw material inventory turnover period	1.0
Less: credit taken from suppliers	(1.5)
Finished goods inventory turnover period	1.0
Receivable's payment period	2.0
Cash cycle	2.5

There would be a gap of 2½ months between paying cash for raw materials and receiving cash (including profits) from receivables. A few dates might clarify this point. Suppose the firm purchases its raw materials on 1 January. The sequence of events would then be as follows.

	Date
Purchase of raw materials	1 Jan
Issue of materials to production (one month after purchase)	1 Feb
Payment made to suppliers (1½ months after purchase)	15 Feb
Sale of finished goods (one month after production begins)	1 Mar
Receipt of cash from receivables (two months after sale)	1 May

The cash cycle is the period of 2½ months from 15 February, when payment is made to suppliers, until 1 May, when cash is received from customers.

3.4 Turnover periods

A **'turnover'** period is an (average) length of time.

(a) In the case of inventory turnover, it is the length of time an item of inventory is held in stores before it is used.

   (i) A raw materials inventory turnover period is the length of time raw materials are held before being issued to the production department.

   (ii) A work in progress turnover period is the length of time it takes to turn raw materials into finished goods in the factory.

   (iii) A finished goods inventory turnover period is the length of time that finished goods are held in a warehouse before they are sold.

   (iv) When a firm buys goods and re-sells them at a profit, the inventory turnover period is the time between their purchase and their resale.

(b) The receivables' turnover period, or debt collection period, is the length of the credit period taken by customers – it is the time between the sale of an item and the receipt of cash for the sale from the customer.

(c) Similarly, the payables' turnover period, or period of credit taken from suppliers, is the length of time between the purchase of materials and the payment to suppliers.

Turnover periods can be calculated from information in a firm's income statement and statement of financial position.

Inventory turnover periods are calculated as follows.

(a) Raw materials: $\dfrac{\text{(Average) raw material inventories held}}{\text{Total raw material consumed in one year}} \times 12 \text{ months}$

(b) Work in progress (the length of the production period):

$$\dfrac{\text{(Average) WIP}}{\text{Total cost of production in the year}} \times 12 \text{ months}$$

(c) Finished goods: $\dfrac{\text{(Average) inventories}}{\text{Total cost of goods sold in one year}} \times 12 \text{ months}$

(d) Inventories of items bought for re-sale: $\dfrac{\text{(Average) inventories}}{\substack{\text{Total (materials) cost of goods} \\ \text{bought and sold in one year}}} \times 12 \text{ months}$

The word 'average' is put in brackets because although it is strictly correct to use average values, it is more common to use the value of inventories shown in a single statement of financial position – at one point in time – to estimate the turnover periods. But if available use opening and closing balances divided by two.

3.5 Example

A company buys goods costing $620,000 in one year and uses goods costing $600,000 in production (in regular monthly quantities) and the cost of material in inventory at 1 January is $100,000.

Solution

The inventory turnover period could be calculated as:

$$\frac{\$100,000}{\$600,000} \times 12 \text{ months} = 2 \text{ months}$$

In other words, inventories are bought two months before they are used or sold.

3.6 Trade receivables collection period

Formula to learn

The debt collection period is calculated as:

$$\frac{\text{Average receivables}}{\text{Annual credit sales}} \times 12 \text{ months}$$

3.7 Example

If a company sells goods for $1,200,000 per annum in regular monthly quantities, and if receivables are $150,000.

Solution

The trade receivables collection period is

$$\frac{\$150,000}{\$1,200,000} \times 12 \text{ months} = 1.5 \text{ months}$$

In other words, receivables will pay for goods 1½ months on average after the time of sale.

3.8 Trade payables payment period

Formula to learn

The period of credit taken from suppliers is calculated as:

$$\frac{\text{Average trade payables}}{\text{Total purchases in one year}} \times 12 \text{ months}$$

Notice that the payables are compared with materials bought whereas for raw material inventory turnover, raw material inventories are compared with materials used in production. This is a small, but very significant difference.

3.9 Example

For example, if a company sells goods for $600,000 and makes a gross profit of 40% on sales, and if the amount of trade payables is $30,000.

Solution

The period of credit taken from the suppliers is:

$$\frac{£30,000}{(60\% \text{ of } £600,000)} \times 12 \text{ months} = 1 \text{ month}$$

In other words, suppliers are paid in the month following the purchase of goods.

Legion's 20X4 accounts show the following.

	$
Sales	360,000
Cost of goods sold	180,000
Inventories	30,000
Receivables	75,000
Trade payables	45,000

Calculate the length of the cash cycle.

Answer

Inventory turnover	Debt collection period	Credit taken from suppliers
$\dfrac{30,000}{180,000} \times 12$	$\dfrac{75,000}{360,000} \times 12$	$\dfrac{45,000}{180,000} \times 12$
= 2 months	= 2^{1}/2 months	= 3 months

The cash cycle is

	Months
Inventory turnover period	2.0
Credit taken from suppliers	(3.0)
Debt collection period	2.5
Cash cycle	1.5

In this example, Legion pays its suppliers one month after the inventories have been sold, since the inventory turnover is two months but credit taken is three months.

3.10 Turnover periods and the total amount of working capital

If the inventory turnover period gets longer or if the debt collection period gets longer, the total amount of inventories or of receivables will increase. Similarly, if the period of credit taken from the suppliers gets shorter, the amount of payables will become smaller. The effect of these changes would be to increase the size of working capital (ignoring bank balances or overdrafts).

3.11 Example

Suppose that a company has annual sales of $480,000 (in regular monthly quantities, all on credit) and a materials cost of sales of $300,000. (*Note.* A 'materials cost of sales' is the cost of materials in the cost of sales.)

(a)   If the inventory turnover period is 2 months, the debt collection period 1 month and the period of credit taken from suppliers is 2 months, the company's working capital (ignoring cash) would be

		$
Inventories	(2/12 × $300,000)	50,000
Receivables	(1/12 × $480,000)	40,000
		90,000
Payables	(2/12 × $300,000)	(50,000)
		40,000

The cash cycle would be (2 + 1 − 2) = 1 month.

(b)   Now if the inventory turnover period is extended to 3 months and the debt collection period to 2 months, and if the payment period for purchases from suppliers is reduced to one month, the company's working capital (ignoring cash) would be

		$
Inventory	(3/12 × $300,000)	75,000
Receivables	(2/12 × $480,000)	80,000
		155,000
Payables	(1/12 × $300,000)	(25,000)
		130,000

and the cash cycle would be $(3 + 2 - 1) = 4$ months.

3.12 Working capital and the cash cycle

If we ignore the possible effects on the bank balance or bank overdraft, (which are themselves included in working capital) it should be seen that a lengthening of the cash cycle will result in a larger volume of working capital.

If the volume of working capital required by a business varies with the length of the cash cycle, it is worth asking the question: 'Is there an ideal length of cash cycle and an ideal volume of working capital?'

Obviously, inventories, receivables and payables should be managed efficiently.

(a)   Inventories should be sufficiently large to meet the demand for inventory items when they are needed, but they should not be allowed to become excessive.

(b)   Receivables should be allowed a reasonable credit period, but overdue payments should be 'chased up', to obviate the risk of bad debts.

(c)   Suppliers should be asked to allow a reasonable period of credit and the firm should make use of the credit periods offered by them.

4 Liquidity

FAST FORWARD

Liquidity may be more important than profitability when looking at whether or not a business can continue to operate.

Key term

The word **'liquid'** means 'readily converted into cash' and a firm's **liquidity** is its ability to convert its assets into cash to meet all the demands for payments when they fall due.

4.1 Current assets and liabilities

The most liquid asset, of course, is cash itself (or a bank balance). The next most liquid assets are short-term investments (stocks and shares) because these can be sold quickly for cash should this be necessary.

Receivables are fairly liquid assets because they should be expected to pay their bills in the near future. Inventories are the least liquid current asset because they must first be sold (perhaps on credit) and the customers given a credit period in which to pay before they can be converted into cash.

Current liabilities are items which must be paid for in the near future. When payment becomes due, enough cash must be available. The managers of a business must therefore make sure that a regular supply of cash comes in (from current assets) at all times to meet the regular flow of payments it is necessary to provide for.

As the previous description of the cash cycle might suggest, the amount of current assets and current liabilities for any business will affect its liquidity. In other words, the volume of working capital helps us to judge the firm's ability to pay its bills.

4.2 The financing of working capital and business assets

Example

STATEMENT OF FINANCIAL POSITION AS AT 31 DECEMBER 20X6

	$'000	$'000
Non-current assets		
Goodwill		50
Premises		700
Plant and machinery		300
		1,050
Current costs		
Inventories	99	
Receivables	50	
Cash in hand	1	
		150
		1,200
Capital and reserves		
Share capital		400
Reserves		500
		900
Long-term liabilities		
Loan stock		200
Current liabilities		
Bank overdraft	20	
Trade payables	50	
Taxation due	30	
		100
		1,200

The **long-term funds** of the business are share capital and reserves of $900,000 and loan stock of $200,000, making $1,100,000 in total. These funds help to finance the business and we can calculate that these funds are being used as follows.

	$
To 'finance' goodwill	50,000
To finance premises	700,000
To finance plant and machinery	300,000
To finance working capital	50,000
	1,100,000

Working capital is therefore financed by the long-term funds of the business.

If a company has more current liabilities than current assets, it has **negative** working capital. This means that to some extent, current liabilities are helping to finance the non-current assets of the business. In the following statement of financial position, working capital is negative (net current liabilities of $20,000).

STATEMENT OF FINANCIAL POSITION AS AT ....

	$
Non-current assets	220,000
Current assets	60,000
	280,000
Capital and reserves	200,000
Current liabilities	80,000
	280,000

The non current assets of $220,000 are financed by share capital and reserves ($200,000), but also by net current liabilities ($20,000). Since current liabilities are debts which will soon have to be paid, the company is faced with more payments than it can find the cash from liquid assets to pay for. This means that the firm will have to

(a) Sell off some non-current assets to get the cash.

(b) Borrow money to overcome its cash flow problems, by offering any unmortgaged property as security for the borrowing.

(c) Be forced into 'bankruptcy' or 'liquidation' by the payables who cannot be paid.

Clearly, a business must be able to pay its bills on time and this means that to have negative working capital would be financially unsound and dangerous. To be safe, a business should have current assets in excess of current liabilities, not just equality with current assets and current liabilities of exactly the same amount.

The next question to ask then is whether there is an 'ideal' amount of working capital which it is prudent to have. In other words, is there an ideal relationship between the amount of current assets and the amount of current liabilities? Should a minimum proportion of current assets be financed by the long-term funds of a business?

These questions cannot be answered without a hard-and-fast rule, but the relative size of current assets and current liabilities are measured by so-called **liquidity ratios**.

4.3 Liquidity ratios

There are two common liquidity ratios.

(a) The current ratio or working capital ratio
(b) The quick ratio or acid test ratio

Key term

The **current ratio** or **working capital ratio** is the ratio of current assets to current liabilities.

A 'prudent' current ratio is sometimes said to be 2:1. In other words, current assets should be twice the size of current liabilities. This is a rather simplistic view though, and particular attention needs to be paid to certain matters.

(a) Bank overdrafts: these are technically repayable on demand, and therefore must be classified as current liabilities. However, many companies have semi-permanent overdrafts in which case the likelihood of their having to be repaid in the near future is remote. It would also often be relevant to know a company's overdraft limit – this may give a truer indication of liquidity than a current or quick ratio.

(b) Are the year-end figures typical of the year as a whole? This is particularly relevant in the case of seasonal businesses. For example, many large retail companies choose an accounting year end following soon after the January sales and their statements of financial position show a higher level of cash and lower levels of inventory and payables than would be usual at any other time in the year.

In practice, many businesses operate with a much lower current ratio and in these cases, the best way to judge their liquidity would be to look at the current ratio at different dates over a period of time. If the trend is towards a lower current ratio, we would judge that the liquidity position is getting steadily worse.

Left page

Formula to learn

The two most usual methods of measuring gearing are

(a) $$\frac{\text{Prior charge capital (long} - \text{term loans and prefere...})}{\text{Equity (ordinary shares plus reserves...)}}$$

   (i) A business is low-geared if the gearing...

   (ii) It is neutrally-geared if the gearing is ex...

   (iii) It is high-geared if the gearing is more t...

(b) $$\frac{\text{Prior charge capital (long} - \text{term loans and prefere...})}{\text{Total long} - \text{term capital}}$$

5.1 High and low gearing

A business is now low-geared if gearing is less than 5...
exactly 50% and high-geared if it exceeds 50%.

Low gearing means that there is more equity finance i...
means the opposite – prior charge capital exceeds the...

5.2 Example

A numerical example might be helpful.

Draught Co, the company in paragraph 2.19, has a ge...

$$\frac{\$200,000 \quad \text{(loan stock plus preference shares)}}{\$400,000 \quad \text{(ordinary shares plus reserves)}} \times 10...$$

5.3 Why is gearing important?

Gearing can be important when a company wants to r...
might find that it is difficult to raise a loan. Would-be...
provide a fair proportion of the total capital for the bus...
be worried that profits are not sufficient to meet future...

5.4 When does gearing become exce...

Unfortunately, there is no hard and fast answer to this...
country (eg average gearing is higher among compani...
the individual company within the industry. The more...

5.5 Advantages of gearing

The advantages of gearing (ie of using debt capital) ar...

(a) Debt capital is cheaper.

   (i) The reward (interest or preferenc...
terms if there is inflation. Ordinar...

   (ii) The reward required by debt-hold...
capital is often secured on compa...

Right page

For example, if the liquidity ratios of two firms A and B are as follows.

	1 Jan	1 Apr	1 July	1 Oct
Firm A	1.2 : 1	1.2 : 1	1.2 : 1	1.2 : 1
Firm B	1.3 : 1	1.2 : 1	1.1 : 1	1.0 : 1

we could say that firm A is maintaining a stable liquidity position, whereas firm B's liquidity is deteriorating. We would then begin to question firm B's continuing ability to pay its bills. A bank for instance, would need to think carefully before granting any request from firm B for an extended overdraft facility.

It is dangerous however to leap to conclusions when analysing ratios. As well as seasonal variations, it is possible that there is not so much overtrading as deliberately selling hard in order to build up business over time. What looks like a poor statement of financial position in one year may develop later into a much bigger and better one.

The quick ratio is used when we take the view that inventories take a long time to get ready for sale, and then there may be some delay in getting them sold, so that inventories are not particularly liquid assets. If this is the case, a firm's liquidity depends more heavily on the amount of receivables, short-term investments and cash that it has to match its current liabilities.

Key term

> The **quick ratio** is the ratio of current assets **excluding inventories** to current liabilities.

A 'prudent' quick ratio is 1:1. In practice, many businesses have a lower quick ratio (eg 0.5:1), and the best way of judging a firm's liquidity would be to look at the trend in the quick ratio over a period of time. The quick ratio is also known as the **liquidity ratio** and as the **acid test ratio.**

4.4 Example: working capital ratios

The cash balance of Wing Co has declined significantly over the last 12 months. The following financial information is provided.

	Year to 31 December	
	20X2	20X3
	$	$
Sales	573,000	643,000
Purchases of raw materials	215,000	264,000
Raw materials consumed	210,000	256,400
Cost of goods manufactured	435,000	515,000
Cost of goods sold	420,000	460,000
Receivables	97,100	121,500
Payables	23,900	32,500
Inventories: raw materials	22,400	30,000
work in progress	29,000	34,300
finished goods	70,000	125,000

All purchases and sales were made on credit.

Required

Analyse the above information, which should include calculations of the cash operating cycle (the time lag between making payment to suppliers and collecting cash from customers) for 20X2 and 20X3.

Notes

(a) Assume a 360 day year for the purpose of your calculations and that all transactions take place at an even rate.

(b) All calculations are to be made to the nearest day.

Solution

The information should be analysed in as many way[s...]
relevant calculations would seem to be as follows.

(i)

      Sales
      Cost of goods sold
      Gross profit

      Gross profit percentage

(ii)   Size of working capital and liquidity ratios, [...]

      Receivables
      Inventories: raw materials
                work in progress
                finished goods

      Payables
      Working capital (ignoring cash or overdraft[)...]

      Current ratio

(iii) *Turnover periods*

                                20X2

Raw materials in inventory $\dfrac{22,400}{210,000} \times$ [...]

Work in progress $\dfrac{29,000}{435,000} \times$ [...]

Finished goods inventory $\dfrac{70,000}{420,000} \times$ [...]

Receivables' collection period $\dfrac{97,100}{573,000} \times$ [...]

Payables' payment period $\dfrac{23,900}{215,000} \times$ [...]

Cash cycle

5 Gearing

FAST FORWARD

Companies are financed by different types of capita[l...]
Gearing measures the degree to which the compan[y...]

Key term

Gearing is a method of comparing how much of th[e...]
shares and reserves) and how much is provided by [...]
dividend before ordinary shareholders can have a [...]

(iii)   Payments of interest attract tax relief, whereas ordinary (or preference) dividends do not.

(b)   Debt capital does not normally carry voting rights, but ordinary shares usually do. The issue of debt capital therefore leaves pre-existing voting rights unchanged.

(c)   If profits are rising, and interest is fixed, ordinary shareholders will benefit from the growth in profits.

The main disadvantage of gearing is that if profits fall even slightly, the profit available to shareholders will fall at a greater rate.

6 Items in company accounts formats

Question

You are given summarised results of an electrical engineering business, as follows.

INCOME STATEMENT

	Year ended	
	31.12.X7	*31.12.X6*
	$'000	$'000
Turnover	60,000	50,000
Cost of sales	42,000	34,000
Gross profit	18,000	16,000
Operating expenses	15,500	13,000
	2,500	3,000
Interest payable	2,200	1,300
Profit before taxation	300	1,700
Taxation	350	600
(Loss) profit after taxation	(50)	1,100
Dividends paid	600	600

STATEMENT OF FINANCIAL POSITION

	$'000	$'000
Non-current assets		
Intangible	850	–
Tangible	12,000	11,000
	12,850	11,000
Current assets		
Inventories	14,000	13,000
Receivables	16,000	15,000
Bank and cash	500	500
	43,350	39,500
Capital and reserves		
Share capital	1,300	1,300
Share premium	3,300	3,300
Revaluation reserve	2,000	2,000
Retained earnings	6,750	7,400
	13,350	14,000
Current liabilities	24,000	20,000
Non-current liabilities	6,000	5,500
	43,350	39,500

Required

Prepare a table of the following 12 ratios, calculated for both years, clearly showing the figures used in the calculations.

Current ratio
Quick assets ratio
Inventory turnover in days
Receivables turnover in days
Payables turnover in days
Gross profit %
Net profit % (before taxation)
ROCE
Gearing

Answer

	20X7	20X6
Current ratio	$\dfrac{30,500}{24,000} = 1.27$	$\dfrac{28,500}{20,000} = 1.43$
Quick assets ratio	$\dfrac{16,500}{24,000} = 0.69$	$\dfrac{15,500}{20,000} = 0.78$
Inventory (number of days held)	$\dfrac{14,000}{42,000} \times 365 = 122$ days	$\dfrac{13,000}{34,000} \times 365 = 140$ days
Receivables (number of days outstanding)	$\dfrac{16,000}{60,000} \times 365 = 97$ days	$\dfrac{15,000}{50,000} \times 365 = 109$ days
Payables (number of days outstanding)	$\dfrac{24,000}{42,000} \times 365 = 209$ days	$\dfrac{20,000}{34,000} \times 365 = 215$ days
Gross profit	$\dfrac{18,000}{60,000} = 30\%$	$\dfrac{16,000}{50,000} = 32\%$
Net profit % (before taxation)	$\dfrac{300}{60,000} = 0.5\%$	$\dfrac{1,700}{50,000} = 3.4\%$
ROCE	$\dfrac{2,500}{19,350} = 13\%$	$\dfrac{3,000}{19,500} = 15\%$
Gearing	$\dfrac{6,000}{19,350} = 31\%$	$\dfrac{5,500}{19,500} = 28\%$

Question

Company accounts

Try to get hold of as many sets of published accounts as possible. Study them carefully to familiarise yourself with the format. Try to form your own opinions on how well the companies are doing.

As a morale booster you should repeat this exercise at later stages in your studies. You may be pleasantly surprised at the progress you make!

You must learn these formulae (all mentioned in the syllabus), understand what they indicate and be able to explain what an increase or decrease means.

Current ratio	$\dfrac{\text{Current assets}}{\text{Current liabilities}}$
Quick (acid test) ratio	$\dfrac{\text{Current assets} - \text{inventory}}{\text{Current liabilties}}$
Return on capital employed (ROCE)	$\dfrac{\text{Net profit before interest}}{\text{Total long - term capital}}$
Gearing	$\dfrac{\text{Prior charge capital}}{\text{Total long - term capital}}$
Receivables turnover (trade receivables collection period)	$\dfrac{\text{Receivables}}{\text{Sales per day}}$, ie $\dfrac{\text{Receivables}}{\text{Sales}} \times 365$
Payables turnover (trade payables payment period)	$\dfrac{\text{Payables}}{\text{Purchases per day}}$, ie $\dfrac{\text{Payables}}{\text{Purchases}} \times 365$
Gross profit margin	$\dfrac{\text{Gross profit}}{\text{Sales}}$
Net profit margin	$\dfrac{\text{Net profit}}{\text{Sales}}$
Inventory turnover (inventory days)	$\dfrac{\text{Average (or year - end) inventory}}{\text{Cost of sales per day}}$, ie $\dfrac{\text{Inventory}}{\text{Cost of sales}} \times 365$
Asset turnover	$\dfrac{\text{Sales}}{\text{Net assets (or capital employed)}}$

It is also possible that the assessor may use alternatives to the inventory/payables/receivables turnover ratios.

Rate of receivables turnover	$\dfrac{\text{Sales}}{\text{Receivables}}$ eg $\dfrac{120{,}000}{20{,}000} = 6$ times
Rate of payables turnover	$\dfrac{\text{Purchases}}{\text{Payables}}$ eg $\dfrac{60{,}000}{45{,}000} = 4$ times
Rate of inventory turnover	$\dfrac{\text{Cost of sales}}{\text{Inventory}}$ eg $\dfrac{60{,}000}{20{,}000} = 3$ times

These ratios represent the number of times closing inventory/payables/receivables are used in the course of the year.

Chapter roundup

- Ratio analysis is the calculation of ratios (eg profit margin) from a set of financial statements which is used for comparison with either earlier years or similar businesses to provide information for decision-making.

- The interpretation of financial statements requires a large measure of common sense.

- ROCE can be calculated in a number of ways. Unless told otherwise in the exam, use:

$$\frac{\text{Net profit before tax and interest}}{\text{Average capital employed}}$$

  where capital employed includes long-term finance.

- **Working capital** is the difference between current assets (mainly inventory, receivables and cash) and current liabilities (such as trade payables and a bank overdraft).

- Liquidity may be more important than profitability when looking at whether or not a business can continue to operate.

- Companies are financed by different types of capital and each type expects a return in the form of interest or dividend. Gearing measures the degree to which the company is financed by non-equity investors.

Quick quiz

1   A high profit margin will indicate?

    A   Effective cost control measures
    B   Increases in sales volume
    C   The use of trade discounts to secure extra sales
    D   Increase in suppliers prices

2   Given opening inventory $58,000, closing inventory $62,000, opening payables $15,000, closing payables $25,000, payments to payables $160,000. Calculate the rate of inventory turnover.

    A   2.74 times
    B   2.58 times
    C   2.66 times
    D   2.76 times

3   A lengthening of the cash cycle will result in a smaller volume of working capital. True or false?

4   What does the 'quick ratio' measure?

    A   The rate of change of cash resources
    B   The speed with which receivables are collected
    C   The relationship between current assets (minus inventory) and current liabilities
    D   The relationship between current assets and current liabilities

5   Capital gearing refers to?

    A   The relationship between ordinary shares and reserves
    B   The relationship between equity and preference shares
    C   A method of showing the relationship between prior charge capital and all forms of capital
    D   A method of explaining the risk of non payment of a dividend to the equity shareholders

Answers to quick quiz

1   A   Correct.

     B   Sales volume increases do not necessarily mean high margins. High levels of sales of loss making products would have the opposite effect.

     C   Trade discounts reduce invoiced prices and would tend to have the opposite effect.

     D   This would erode margins.

2   D   Correct: purchases = $160,000 + $25,000 – $15,000 = $170,000

          Cost of goods sold = $68,000 + $170,000 – $72,000 = $166,000

          Average inventory = $60,000, inventory turnover = $\dfrac{\$166,000}{\$60,000}$ = 2.76 times

     A   If average inventory is unobtainable, the use of average inventory and purchases will give an acceptable answer.

     B   This is payments divided by closing inventory.

     C   This is payments dividend by average inventory.

3   False

4   C   Correct, inventory is excluded because it has to be sold to create a receivable balance.
     A   Incorrect.
     B   Incorrect, this is the receivable collection period.
     D   Incorrect, this is the current ratio.

5   C   Correct, there is no single accepted definition but the key point is to compare outside borrowings with internally provided finance.

     A   Incorrect.

     B   Incorrect.

     D   The ordinary shareholders are always at risk, gearing is useful for the providers of debt capital as a measure of risk.

Now try the questions below from the Question Bank

Question numbers
93–97

Manufacturing accounts

Introduction

So far in our studies of accounts preparation we have confined ourselves to the accounts of trading organisations. Britain has been called a nation of shopkeepers, but we would be a very hungry nation if no one actually made things. In Section 1 of this chapter we consider the problems of preparing accounting statements for manufacturing firms.

The most obvious difference between a manufacturing and a trading firm is that the former has many more different types of expense. The **purchases** of the trading firm are replaced by the myriad expenses that arise when, for example, a willow tree is converted into a cricket bat. The traditional way of showing the cost of goods produced is the **manufacturing account**.

Topic list	Syllabus references
1 Manufacturing accounts	C (1)

1 Manufacturing accounts

A **manufacturing account** is an account in which the costs of producing finished goods are calculated. It is prepared for internal use.

Direct factory costs are factory costs which change every time an extra unit is made. For example, direct factory wages are wages paid to production workers who are paid per unit made.

Production overheads or **indirect factory costs** are factory costs which do not change every time an extra unit is made. For example, indirect factory wages are wages paid to production managers who are paid the same each month regardless of how many units are made.

Prime cost is raw material costs plus direct factory costs.

1.1 Cost of goods sold

A company's trading account will usually include a cost of goods sold derived as the total of opening inventory plus purchases, less closing inventory. This is particularly suitable for a retail business which buys in goods and sells them on to customers without altering their condition. But for a manufacturing company it would be truer to say that the cost of goods sold is as follows.

	$
Opening inventory of finished goods	X
Plus cost of finished goods produced in the period	X
	X
Less closing inventory of finished goods	(X)
Cost of finished goods sold	X

Assessment focus point

A pro-forma manufacturing account is set out on the next page with illustrative figures. Make sure you learn the format.

MANUFACTURING ACCOUNT
FOR THE YEAR ENDED 31 DECEMBER 20X6

	$	$
Raw materials		
Opening inventory	4,000	
Purchases (net of returns)	207,000	
	211,000	
Less closing inventory	23,000	
		188,000
Direct factory wages		21,000
Prime cost		209,000
Production overhead		
Factory power	4,000	
Plant depreciation	3,000	
Plant maintenance	1,500	
Rent and insurance	2,500	
Light and heat	3,000	
Sundry expenses	5,000	
Factory manager's salary	9,000	
Building depreciation	1,000	
		29,000
Production cost of resources consumed		238,000
Work in progress		
Opening inventory	8,000	
Closing inventory	(17,000)	
Increase in work in progress inventory		(9,000)
Production cost of finished goods produced		229,000

1.2 Work in progress

At the reporting date, there will be work in progress in the production departments, ie work which has been partly converted but which has not yet reached the stage of being finished goods.

The value of this work in progress is the cost of the raw materials, the wages of employees who have worked on it plus a share of overheads. To arrive at the cost of finished goods produced, an increase in work in progress must be deducted from the total production costs. Of course, if the value of work in progress had **fallen** during the period, this fall would be an **increase** in the cost of finished goods produced.

1.3 Example: manufacturing account and income statement

Assessment focus point

> The manufacturing account is needed to calculate the cost of finished goods. This figure is then carried forward into the income statement to replace purchases in the cost of sales calculation.

A manufacturing company has its factory and offices at the same site. Its results for the year to 31 December 20X5 were:

	$
Sales	179,000
Purchases of raw materials	60,000
Direct labour	70,000
Depreciation of equipment	10,000
Rent	5,000

	$
Depreciation of building	2,000
Heating and lighting	3,000
Telephone	2,000
Other manufacturing overheads	2,300
Other administration expenses	2,550
Other selling expenses	1,150

Shared overhead costs are to be apportioned as follows.

	Manufacturing	Administration	Selling
Depreciation of equipment	80%	5%	15%
Rent	50%	30%	20%
Depreciation of building	50%	30%	20%
Heating and lighting	40%	35%	25%
Telephone	–	40%	60%

The values of inventories are as follows.

	At 1 January 20X5	At 31 December 20X5
	$	$
Raw materials	5,000	3,000
Work in progress	4,000	3,000
Finished goods	16,000	18,000

Required

Prepare the manufacturing account and income statement of the company for the period to 31 December 20X5.

Solution

MANUFACTURING ACCOUNT FOR THE YEAR ENDED 31 DECEMBER 20X5

	$	$
Opening inventory of raw materials		5,000
Purchases		60,000
		65,000
Closing inventory of raw materials		3,000
Raw materials used in production		62,000
Direct labour		70,000
Prime cost		132,000
Manufacturing overheads		
Depreciation of equipment (80% of $10,000)	8,000	
Rent (50% of $5,000)	2,500	
Depreciation of building (50% of $2,000)	1,000	
Heating and lighting (40% of $3,000)	1,200	
Other expenses	2,300	
		15,000
Manufacturing costs during the year		147,000
Add opening inventory of work in progress	4,000	
Less closing inventory of work in progress	(3,000)	
Reduction in inventory of work in progress		1,000
Cost of finished goods fully produced, transferred to income statement		148,000

BPP
LEARNING MEDIA

INCOME STATEMENT
FOR THE YEAR ENDED 31 DECEMBER 20X5

	$	$	$
Sales			179,000
Opening inventory of finished goods		16,000	
Cost of finished goods produced		148,000	
		164,000	
Closing inventory of finished goods		18,000	
Cost of goods sold			146,000
Gross profit			33,000
Selling expenses			
Depreciation of equipment (15% of $10,000)	1,500		
Rent (20% of $5,000)	1,000		
Depreciation of building (20% of $2,000)	400		
Heating and lighting (25% of $3,000)	750		
Telephone (60% of $2,000)	1,200		
Other expenses	1,150		
		6,000	
Administration expenses			
Depreciation of equipment (5% of $10,000)	500		
Rent (30% of $5,000)	1,500		
Depreciation of building (30% of $2,000)	600		
Heating and lighting (35% of $3,000)	1,050		
Telephone (40% of $2,000)	800		
Other expenses	2,550		
		7,000	
Net profit			13,000
			20,000

Question
Manufacturing account and income statement

The following information has been extracted from the books of account of the Marsden Manufacturing Company for the year to 30 September 20X4.

	$
Advertising	2,000
Depreciation for the year to 30 September 20X4	
Factory equipment	7,000
Office equipment	4,000
Direct wages	40,000
Factory: insurance	1,000
heat	15,000
indirect materials	5,000
power	20,000
salaries	25,000
Finished goods (at 1 October 20X3)	24,000
Office: electricity	15,000
general expenses	9,000
postage and telephones	2,900
salaries	70,000
Raw material purchases	202,000
Raw material inventory (at 1 October 20X3)	8,000
Sales	512,400
Work in progress (at 1 October 20X3)	12,000

Chapter roundup

- The receipts and payments account is effectively a summary of an organisation's cash book. For small clubs with a few straightforward transactions, this statement may be sufficient. For larger concerns it will be used to prepare an income and expenditure account and statement of financial position.

- An income and expenditure account is the name given to what is effectively the income statement of a non-trading organisation, eg sports clubs, social clubs, societies, charities and so on. The principles of 'accruals' accounting (the matching concept) are applied to income and expenditure accounts in the same way as for income statements.

- In a non-trading organisation the result for the year is described as a surplus or deficit, not a profit or loss, and the capital of the organisation is known as the accumulated fund.

- Netting off expenditure against income for like items means that where some sources of income have associated costs, the net surplus or deficit should be shown in the income and expenditure account.

- Before looking at an example of an income and expenditure account we need to look at each of the following items in some detail.

  - Membership subscriptions
  - Bar trading account
  - Life membership

- Subscriptions received in advance are treated as a current liability.

- Subscriptions in arrears are treated as a current asset.

1   Three differences between the accounts of a non-trading organisation and those of a business are:

   (1) _____

   (2) _____

   (3) _____

2   If a 'not for profit' organisation does make a surplus it will be?

   A   Credit to capital
   B   Credit to the accumulated fund
   C   Repaid to the contributions or members
   D   Added to the bank account balance

3   A club has 150 members who pay $10 each for membership. The opening subscription receivable was $70 and 5 members had paid subscriptions in advance at the year end. How much money was collected from members?

   A $1,500
   B $1,740
   C $1,620
   D $1,520

4   The assets and liabilities of a social club were (at 31.12.20X1) equipment $1,500, premises $16,000, bar inventory $1,300, bar payables $1,100, managers wage owing $250, subscriptions in arrears $500, prepaid subscriptions $350, cash $1,900. The accumulated fund is:

   A $21,200
   B $19,650
   C $19,500
   D $200,000

1 (1) A non-trading organisation does not make profits, so the income statement is replaced by an income and expenditure account.

   (2) The 'capital' account is the accumulated fund.

   (3) There is no separate trading account.

2 B Correct.
   A Non trading organisations such as clubs and societies refer to their capital as 'accumulated funds'.
   C Incorrect, unless in the unlikely event of the club or society specifying this is to happen.
   D Incorrect.

3 C Correct.

Subscriptions A/C

Balance b/f	70	Bank	1,620
I&E (subscriptions)			
150 × $10	1,500		
Bal c/f 5 × $10	50		
	1,620		1,620

   A Incorrect, you have not adjusted for opening subscriptions in arrears or closing prepaid subscriptions.

   B Incorrect, you have posted subscription income to the credit of the subscription a/c incorrectly.

   D Incorrect, the closing prepayment of subscriptions must be treated as a payable.

4 C Correct, $1,500 + $16,000 + $1,300 − $1,100 − $250 + $500 − $350 + $1,900 = 19,500.
   A Incorrect, this is the amount of the total assets of the club.
   B Incorrect, you have treated the subscriptions incorrectly.
   D Incorrect, you have treated the outstanding wages as an asset.

Now try the questions below from the Question Bank

Question numbers
105–106

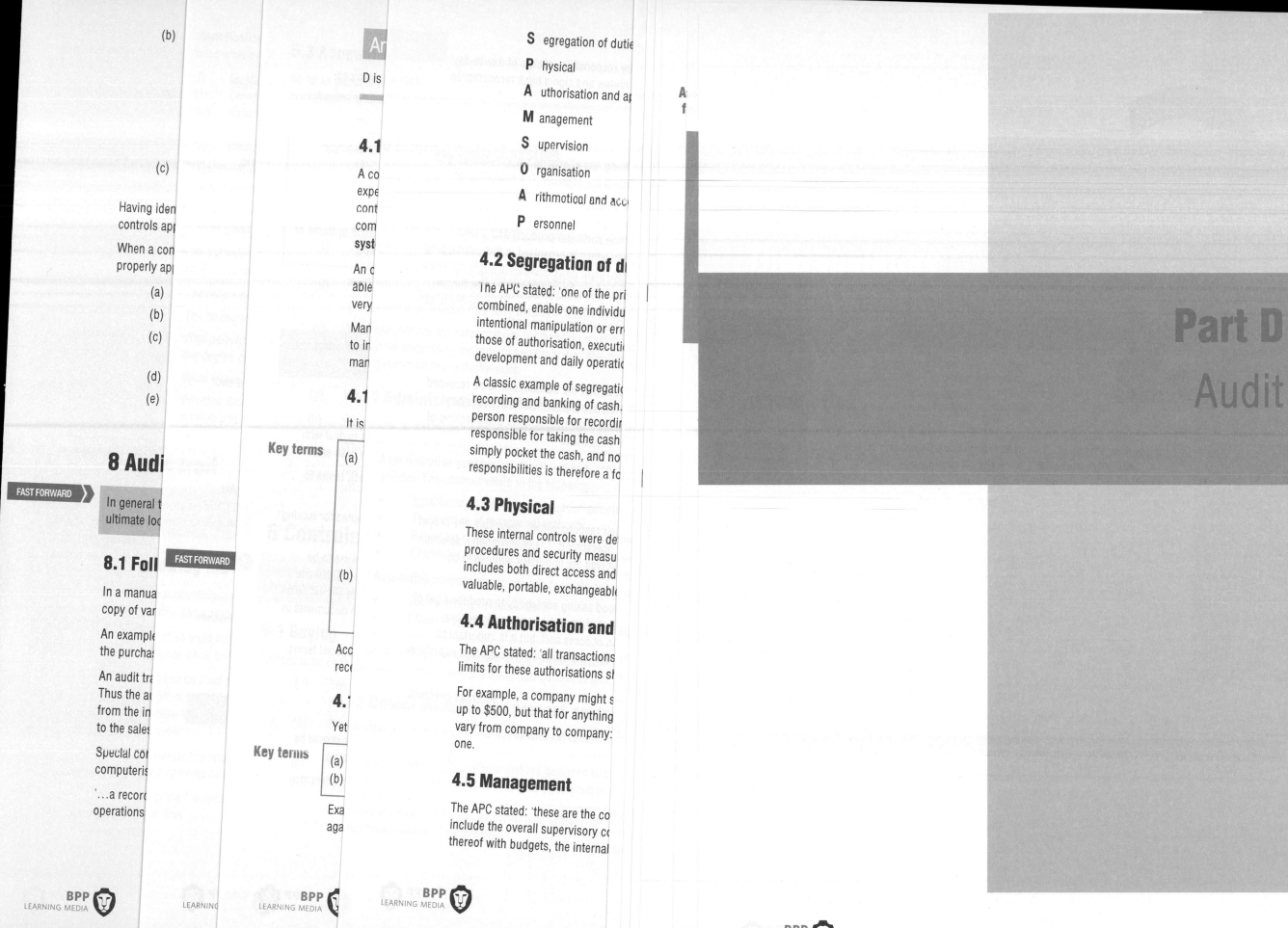

(b)

(c)

Having iden
controls app

When a con
properly app

(a)

(b)

(c)

(d)

(e)

8 Audi

FAST FORWARD

In general t
ultimate loc

8.1 Foll

FAST FORWARD

In a manua
copy of var

An example
the purchas

An audit tra
Thus the au
from the in
to the sales

Special con
computeris

'...a record
operations

S egregation of dutie

P hysical

A uthorisation and a

M anagement

S upervision

O rganisation

A rithmotical and acc

P ersonnel

4.2 Segregation of d

The APC stated: 'one of the pri
combined, enable one individu
intentional manipulation or err
those of authorisation, executi
development and daily operatio

A classic example of segregati
recording and banking of cash.
person responsible for recordir
responsible for taking the cash
simply pocket the cash, and no
responsibilities is therefore a fo

4.3 Physical

These internal controls were de
procedures and security measu
includes both direct access and
valuable, portable, exchangeabl

4.4 Authorisation and

The APC stated: 'all transactions
limits for these authorisations sh

For example, a company might s
up to $500, but that for anything
vary from company to company:
one.

4.5 Management

The APC stated: 'these are the co
include the overall supervisory c
thereof with budgets, the internal

Key terms

(a)

(b)

Key terms

(a)

(b)

Part D
Audit

An audit trail should ideally be provided so that every transaction on a file contains a unique reference back to the original source of the input, for example, a sales system transaction record should hold a reference to the customer order, delivery note and invoice.

Where master file records are updated several times, or from several sources, the provision of a satisfactory audit trail is more difficult but some attempt should nevertheless be made to provide one.

Question
Audit trail

Why is it important that all transactions should leave an audit trail?

A   So every transaction is posted
B   So every transaction can be traced through the system
C   So every transaction is authorised
D   So every transaction can be summarised

Answer

B. So every transaction can be traced from source documents and day books through to final postings to the ledgers.

9 The detection and prevention of fraud

Key term

In *Derry v Peek*, **fraud** was defined as: 'a false representation of fact made with the knowledge of its falsity, or without belief in its truth, or recklessly careless, whether it be true or false'.

The auditing guideline concerns financial fraud, and the definition runs as follows:

'The word 'irregularities' is used to refer to intentional distortions of financial statements, for whatever purpose, and to misappropriations of assets, whether or not accompanied by distortions of financial statements. Fraud is one type of irregularity. The word 'fraud' is used to refer to irregularities involving the use of criminal deception to obtain an unjust or illegal advantage.'

FAST FORWARD

In internal auditing, detection of fraud is an important objective. Auditors should be aware of the common types of fraud and should be particularly watchful when internal controls are poor.

9.1 Types of fraud

Give an employee responsibility, and he may manage the resources under his control dishonestly. The incidence of financial fraud, particularly in a computer environment, is increasing fast. This trend, together with the increasing sophistication of fraudsters, creates difficult problems for management and for internal auditors.

The mere presence of internal auditors will serve to discourage fraudsters for fear of being discovered, but the public's expectations go much further.

The profession has responded in a number of ways, not least the issue of the Auditing Practices Board's standard ISA 240 *The auditor's responsibilities relating to fraud in an audit of financial statements* (October 2009).

If the interr
or in writin

The interna
work by ch

**Assessment
focus point**

As you will see later in this
is called **exception reporti**
an internal auditors report

3.5 Auditing stand

Key term

Auditing standards and gu
Auditing Practices Commit
internal audit and used to c
of internal control they sho

4 Internal cont

FAST FORWARD

The eight types of internal c

4.1 Internal contro

One of the main tasks of the
whether the system's **intern**
recommend improvements.

An **internal control system** i
(Cadbury Committee) as:

Key term

'The whole system of **contro**

(a)   effective and efficient
(b)   internal financial cont
(c)   compliance with laws

The Cadbury Code is concern
financial control'. This is defi

'the internal controls establis

(a)   the safeguardir
(b)   the maintenanc
        business or for

These definitions are fairly bro
organisation is given in the ap
eight types of control listed (o

6.2 Go

Factors t

(a

(l

(

8.3 A

Factors

(a

5 Controls o

5.1 Setting

Que

You sho
which y
questior

(a)   V
(b)   I

7 Ev

FAST FORWARD

Internal

7.1 D

The eva

BPP
LEARNING MEDIA

The auditors will best be able to detect frauds if they are knowledgeable (not experienced!) in the most common methods of fraud. These are as follows.

- Ghost employees on the payroll
- Miscasting of the payroll
- Stealing unclaimed wages
- Collusion with external parties
- Teeming and lading
- Altering cheques after signature
- Inflating expense claims
- Using the company's assets for personal gain
- Stealing fully depreciated assets
- Issuing false credit notes or fraudulently writing off debts
- Failing to record all sales

Ghost employees. These are imaginary employees for whom the wages department prepare wage packets which are distributed amongst the fraudsters. This type of fraud arises when there is extensive reliance on casual workers, and minimal record keeping for such workers. Inflated overtime claims can also result from poor time recording systems. Such frauds can be detected from a review of the numbers of employees required to achieve a standard amount of work. If at some times of the year a larger number appear to be required, there may be something amiss. Scrutiny of signatures given as proof of receipt of wages should also be made.

Miscasting of the payroll. This fraud often succeeds due to its simplicity. If there are twenty employees, each to be paid $100, then the computer program for the payroll could be adjusted so that an extra $50 is added to the total added up for the amounts to be paid. Thus management approve a payment of $2,050 for the period's wages, each employee gets his $100 and the fraudster collects his extra $50. Manual payroll systems can be manipulated in a similar way. When employees are paid in cash, this type of fraud can be hard to trace and all too easy to perpetrate.

Stealing **unclaimed wages** is also common. This is effectively confined to wages paid in cash and can occur when an employee leaves without notice or is away sick. In the case of a subsequent claim for unpaid wages, it could be claimed that the cash in the original pay packet was paid back into the bank.

Collusion with external parties could involve suppliers, customers or their staff. Possible frauds are overcharging on purchase invoices, undercharging on sales invoices or the sale of confidential information (eg customer lists, expansion plans) to a competitor. Management should watch out for unusual discounts or commissions being given or taken, or for an excessive zeal on the part of an employee to handle all business with a particular company.

Teeming and lading is a 'rolling' fraud rather than a 'one-off' fraud. It occurs when a clerk has the chance to misappropriate payments from receivables or to payables. Cash received by the company is borrowed by the cashier rather than being kept as petty cash or banked. (It is also possible, although riskier and more difficult to organise, to misappropriate cheques made payable to the company.) When the cashier knows that a reconciliation is to be performed, or audit visit planned, he pays the money back so that everything appears satisfactory at that point, but after the audit the teeming and lading starts again. Surprise visits by auditors and independent checking of cash balances should discourage this fraud.

A common fraud arising when one employee has sole control of the sales ledger and recording debtors' cheques is to pay cheques into a separate bank account, either by forged endorsement or by opening an account in a name similar to the employer's.

The clerk has to allocate cheques or cash received from other receivables against the account of the receivable whose payment was misappropriated. This prevents other staff from asking why the account is still overdue or from sending statements etc to the receivables. However, the misallocation has to continue as long as the money is missing. This fraud, therefore, never really stops. It can be detected by independent verification of receivables balances (eg by writing to them) and by looking at unallocated payments, if the sales ledger is organised to show this. In addition, sending out itemised monthly statements to receivables should act as a deterrent, although in a really elaborate fraud the clerk may be keeping two sets of books, so that the statements show the receivable's own analysis of amounts due and paid off in the month, but do not agree with the books.

Altering cheques and **inflating expense claims** are self-explanatory.

Using the company's assets for personal gain and stealing fully depreciated assets are both encountered in practice. Whether or not the private use of company telephones and photocopiers is a serious matter is up to the company to judge, but it may still be fraudulent. More serious examples include the sale by employees of unused time on the computer, which is a growing fraud.

Another way of avoiding detection when cash and cheques received from debtors have been misappropriated is to **issue a credit note** which is not sent to the customer (who has paid his account) but is recorded in the books. Again, the issue of itemised statements monthly should show this up, as the customer would query the credit now. However, any company with sufficiently lax controls to allow one clerk both to receive and record cash and additionally to authorise and issue credit notes is unlikely to ensure that someone else issues and follows up statements. A similar tactic is to **write a debt off** as bad to cover up the disappearance of the payment.

A very elaborate fraud may be perpetrated in a business with extremely poor controls over sales recording and minimal segregation of duties. In such circumstances, a dishonest bookkeeper may invoice customers but fail to record the invoices so that the customer's payments never have to be recorded and the misappropriation is not missed.

This type of fraud can occur where a customer is receiving large numbers of invoices from the business every month and so the bookkeeper's failure to record one or two invoices (if detected by auditors or his superiors) is simply put down to incompetence rather than fraud.

A warning sign here is the perception by customers that 'your accounts department is a mess ... always getting things wrong ... we've given up trying to get our account right...'.

9.2 The role of the internal auditors

The internal auditors should start their work by identifying the areas of the business most susceptible to fraud. These will include areas where cash is involved, and the other areas where the auditors' judgement is that the internal controls are insufficient to safeguard the assets.

The existence of a properly functioning system of internal controls will diminish the incidence of frauds, so the auditors' opinion on the internal control system is of fundamental importance.

Whenever a fraud is discovered, they should judge whether a weakness in internal controls has been highlighted, and if so what changes are needed.

9.3 Prevention of fraud

Fraud will only be prevented successfully if potential fraudsters perceive the risk of detection as being high, and if personnel are adequately screened before employment and given no incentive to turn against the company once employed. The following safeguards should therefore be implemented.

(a) A good internal control system.
(b) Continuous supervision of all employees.
(c) Surprise audit visits.
(d) Thorough personnel procedures.

The work of employees must be monitored as this will increase the perceived risk of being discovered. Actual results must regularly be compared against budgeted results, and employees should be asked to explain significant variances.

Surprise audit visits are a valuable contribution to preventing fraud. If a cashier is carrying out a teeming and lading fraud and is told that an audit visit is due the following week, he may be able to square up the books before the visit so that the auditors will find nothing wrong. But if the threat of a surprise visit is constantly present, the cashier will not be able to carry out a teeming and lading fraud without the risk of being discovered, and this risk is usually sufficient to prevent the fraud.

The auditors do not need to carry out any sophisticated audit tests during their surprise visit. There are stories of internal auditors arriving without warning, and taking all the books into a room of their own to read the newspaper for an hour – but the fraud deterrent effect on the employee is highly significant, because the employee thinks that every figure is being checked.

Finally, personnel procedures must be adequate to prevent the occurrence of frauds.

(a)   Whenever a fraud is discovered, the fraudster should be dismissed and the police should be informed. Too often an employee is 'asked to resign' and then moves on to a similar job where the fraud is repeated, often because management fear loss of face or investor confidence. This is a self-defeating policy.

(b)   All new employees should be required to produce adequate references from their previous employers.

(c)   If an employee's lifestyle changes dramatically, explanations should be sought.

(d)   Every employee must be made to take his annual holiday entitlement. Sometimes in practice the employee who is 'so dedicated that he never takes a holiday' is in fact not taking his leave for fear of his fraud being discovered by his replacement worker while he is away.

(e)   Pay levels should be adequate and working conditions of a reasonable standard. If employees feel that they are being paid an unfairly low amount or 'exploited', they may look for ways to supplement their pay dishonestly.

9.4 Management fraud

So far, this chapter has concentrated on employee fraud. However, arguably more serious (and very much more difficult to prevent and detect) is the growing problem of management fraud.

While employee fraud is usually undertaken purely for the employee's financial gain, management fraud is often undertaken to improve the company's apparent performance, to reduce tax liabilities or to improve manager's promotion prospects.

Managers are often in a position to override internal controls and to intimidate their subordinates into collusion or turning a blind eye. This makes it difficult to detect such frauds. In addition, where the company is benefiting financially rather than the manager, it can be difficult to persuade staff that any dishonesty is involved.

This clash of interest between loyalty to an employer and professional integrity can be difficult to resolve and can compromise an internal auditor's independence.

Management fraud often comes to light after a take-over or on a change of audit staff or practices. Its consequences can be far reaching for the employing company in damaging its reputation or because it results in legal action. Because management usually have access to much larger sums of money than more lowly employees, the financial loss to the company can be immense.

Chapter roundup

- It is important to distinguish between ownership and stewardship.

- External auditors report to the members of the company on whether, in their opinion, the annual statutory accounts give a true and fair view. Their duties are imposed by statute and they are not employees of the company. Under International Accounting Standards, auditors report on 'fair presentation'.

- 'True and fair' is not defined in company law or accounting standards. The words are used together rather than separately and the term is generally taken to mean 'reasonably accurate and free from bias or distortion'. Under IAS, the term is 'fair presentation'.

- Internal auditors are employees of the company whose duties are fixed by management and who report to management.

- The scope of an internal audit varies widely and may range from systems review to implementation of corporate policies, plans and processes.

- Contrary to popular belief, it is not the responsibility of external auditors to detect fraud; they are merely obliged to plan their audit tests so that they have a reasonable expectation of detecting fraud. It is the responsibility of the directors to set up an adequate system of internal control to deter and expose fraud. Internal audit is one type of internal control.

- The eight types of internal control can be remembered by using the mnemonic SPAMSOAP.

- There are three separate elements into which sales accounting controls may be divided. They are selling (authorisation), goods outwards (custody) and accounting (recording).

- There are also three separate elements into which accounting controls may be divided in the consideration of purchase procedures. They are buying (authorisation), receipt of goods (custody) and accounting (recording).

- Internal controls need to be evaluated for adequacy and risk.

- In general terms an audit trail is a means by which an auditor can follow through a transaction from its origin to its ultimate location or vice versa.

- In internal auditing, detection of fraud is an important objective. Auditors should be aware of the common types of fraud and should be particularly watchful when internal controls are poor.

1   The auditor's report states whether the financial statements give a 'true and fair' view. True and fair has never been statutorily defined. True or false?

2   To whom should the head of internal audit report in a large company?

   A   The finance director
   B   The chief accountant
   C   The chairman of the board of directors
   D   The external auditors

3   Which of the following statements concerning the status of an external auditor is incorrect?

   A   All companies must appoint external auditors
   B   The duties of an auditor are defined by the Companies Act 2006
   C   The auditor gives an opinion on the financial statements
   D   The auditor reports to the members of the company

4   Which of the following procedures is unlikely to be encountered in following through an 'audit trail' in a computerised accounting system?

   A   The authorisation of input documents
   B   One for one checking of master file amendments
   C   Output being completely checked against input data in a system producing budgetary control reports
   D   Authorisation of changes to a computer program

5   What is a 'teeming and lading fraud'?

   A   Stealing cash

   B   Colluding with external partners to submit false invoices

   C   Stealing cash, concealing the theft by delaying bankings or making good the shortage by transfers from other sources

   D   Altering cheques and cash receipt records to record lesser amounts and pocketing the difference

1   True

2   C   Correct. This is ideal, an alternative would be to report to the board or an audit committee.

     A   Independence will be compromised and recommendations possibly diluted.

     B   The chief accountant may lack authority to implement the needed changes following an internal audit review and independence may be compromised.

     D   The external auditors must not be involved in executive decisions within a client, otherwise their independence could be compromised.

3   A   Correct. Small limited companies and unincorporated businesses or partnerships need not have an external audit.

4   C   Correct. It is more usual to find output on a exceptions basis, such as the investigation of significant variances in the example given.

     A   A key element of control over input, difficult to achieve in on-line or real-time systems.

     B   An important procedure to preserve the integrity of master file data.

     D   This would be present in the systems documentation.

5   C   Correct. The characteristics of this type of fraud are theft (or 'borrowing') coupled with a scheme to conceal typically involving delayed bankings.

     A   The objective of a teeming and lading fraud is to misappropriate cash, it is how it is concealed which is unique.

     B   This is not a teeming and fraud, although it is a common type of fraud.

     D   This is a straightforward receipts fraud.

Now try the questions below from the Question Bank

Question numbers
112–125

Question bank

1   List 5 user groups who would be interested in financial information about a large public company.

(a) _____

(b) _____

(c) _____

(d) _____

(e) _____   **2 Marks**

2   Which of the following statements is true?

A   Financial accountants provide historical information for internal use
B   Financial accountants provide historical information for external use
C   Financial accountants provide forward looking information for internal use
D   Financial accountants provide forward looking information for external use   **2 Marks**

3   Fill in the missing word.

Management accounting is the preparation of accounting reports for ………………….. use.   **2 Marks**

4   Which of the following statements gives the best definition of the objective of accounting?

A   To provide useful information to users
B   To record, categorise and summarise financial transactions
C   To calculate the taxation due to the government
D   To control the assets, liabilities and profitability of an entity.   **2 Marks**

5   Peter Reid decides he is going to open a bookshop called Easyread, which he does by investing $5,000 on 1 January 20X7. During the first month of Easyread's existence, the following transactions occur.

(a)   Bookshelves are purchased for $1,800.
(b)   Books are purchased for $2,000.
(c)   Half of the books are sold for $1,500 cash.
(d)   Peter draws $200 out of the business for himself.
(e)   Peter's brother John loans $500 to the business.
(f)   Carpets are purchased for $1,000 on credit (to be paid in two months time).
(g)   A bulk order of books worth $400 is sold on credit (to be paid in one month's time) for $600.

Required

Write down the accounting equation after all of these transactions have taken place

Assets	=	Capital	+	Liabilities
_____		_____		_____

2 Marks

6   Which statement is wrong for a statement of financial position to balance?

A   Net assets   =   Proprietor's fund
B   Net assets   =   Capital + profit + drawings
C   Net assets   =   Capital + profit − drawings
D   Non-current assets + net current assets = capital + profit − drawings   **2 Marks**

7 James starts his secondhand car business with $155,000. He spends $80,000 on vehicles. One of them is a $5,000 van which he decides to keep and use in the business. During the first month he pays rent of $500 and sells two cars for a total of $10,000. They had cost $5,000 and he spent $1,000 having them repaired. He has not yet paid the repair bills.

State the accounting equation at the end of the month.

Assets	=	Capital	+	Liabilities
$_____	=	$_____	+	$_____	**2 Marks**

8 Which of the following transactions is capital expenditure and which revenue expenditure? Tick the correct box.

	Capital	Revenue
(a) A bookseller buys a car for its director for $9,000.		
(b) In the first year, the car is depreciated by $900.		
(c) The business buys books for $1,500.		
(d) The business builds an extension for $7,600.		
(e) The original building is repainted, a job costing $1,200.		
(f) A new sales assistant is taken on and his salary in the first year is $10,000.		

2 Marks

9 A business has spent $200 replacing worn out parts on a machine. How should this $200 be treated in the accounts and why?

A   As revenue expenditure because it is repairing a non-current asset
B   As capital expenditure because it is improving a non-current asset
C   As revenue expenditure because it is likely to reoccur
D   As capital expenditure because it is a small amount   **2 Marks**

10 Which of the following costs of Café Edmundo would be classified as capital expenditure?

A   Cost of printing a batch of new menu cards
B   Repainting the restaurant
C   An illuminated sign advertising the business name
D   Knives and forks for the restaurant   **2 Marks**

11 Fill in the two missing words.

Return is a ………………………….. for …………………………… in a business.   **2 Marks**

12 The sales day book lists _____.

The purchase day book lists _____.

The sales returns day book lists _____.

The purchases returns day book lists _____.   **2 Marks**

13 Cash received from customers will be posted as follows:

(a)   Debit receivables/Credit cash
(b)   Debit cash/Credit sales revenue
(c)   Debit cash/Credit receivables
(d)   Debit sales revenue/Credit receivables   **2 Marks**

14 _____ are recorded in day books. The totals of day books are posted by double entry to ledger accounts in the _____ _____.

Individual invoice details in the day books are posted by single entry to accounts in the

_____ _____. **2 Marks**

15 A company uses the imprest system for its petty cash, keeping to a float of $100. Since cash was last drawn, $20 has been paid to the cleaner, $15 has been spent on stationery and $7.50 paid to the milkman. One of the directors has repaid a $12 travel advance given to him several weeks ago.

The amount needed to restore the imprest is _____. **2 Marks**

16 (a) A company has been overcharged by one of its suppliers. They receive a credit note. This is posted as follows:

	DR	CR	
Cash			*Tick the*
Creditor			*correct box*
Purchases			

2 Marks

(b) As they are not making any further purchases, the supplier then sends a refund. This is posted as follows:

	DR	CR	
Cash			*Tick the*
Creditor			*correct box*
Purchases			

2 Marks

17 The total of the sales day-book is recorded in the nominal ledger as:

	Debit	*Credit*
A	Sales Account	Receivables Control Account
B	Receivables Control Account	Receivables
C	Receivables	Receivables Control Account
D	Receivables Control Account	Sales Account

2 Marks

18 Fill in the missing word.

The sales and purchases ledgers are not part of the double entry system. They are .... accounts only. **2 Marks**

19 Which of the following postings from the cashbook payments side is wrong?

A   The total of the cash paid column to the debit of the cash control account.
B   The total of the discounts column to the credit of the discounts received account.
C   The total of the discounts column to the debit of the payables control account.
D   The total of the cash paid column to the credit of the cash control account. **2 Marks**

20   The sales day book total for March of $250 was recorded in the nominal ledger as:

Cr   Sales account
Cr   Receivables account

At 31 December a trial balance was prepared. Would the trial balance balance?

A   Yes
B   No   Credits would exceed debits by 250
C   No   Credits would exceed debits by $500
D   No   Debits would exceed credits by $250   **2 Marks**

21   When a trial balance is prepared the clerk treats purchases of $3,000 as a credit balance. Credits exceed/are
smaller than debits in the trial balance by $_____.   **2 Marks**

22   Fred's trial balance included the following.

	$	$
Purchases	6,000	
Opening inventory	400	
Carriage inwards	200	
Carriage outwards	150	
Sales		12,500

Closing inventory cost $1,000, but it is slightly water damaged. Fred thinks that he can sell it for $1,100 but only
if he spends $200 on repackaging it.

Gross profit is $_____.   **2 Marks**

23   Which accounting concept is being followed in each of these scenarios?

(a)   Including costs in the period in which they are incurred, regardless of when payment is made

_____

(b)   Not changing depreciation policy from one year to the next _____

(c)   Providing for liabilities which are expected to arise _____   **2 Marks**

24   Which basic accounting concept is being followed when an allowance is made for bad debts and receivables?

A   Accruals
B   Consistency
C   Going concern
D   Prudence   **2 Marks**

25   Fill in the four missing words.

The accruals basis of accounting requires that, in computing profit, amounts are included in the accounts in the
period when they are ……………………………… or …………………………….., not
……………………………… or ………………………………… .   **2 Marks**

26   Where there is tension between the concepts of accruals and prudence

A   Accruals must prevail
B   Seek help from external auditors
C   A neutral approach must be adopted that ensures a fair presentation
D   Prudence must prevail   **2 Marks**

27   Fill in the missing word.

The double entry system of bookkeeping is based on the concept of ....   **2 Marks**

28   Making allowances for receivables and valuing inventory on the same basis in each accounting period are examples of which accounting concepts?

	Allowance for receivables	Inventory valuation
A	Accruals	Consistency
B	Accruals	Going concern
C	Prudence	Consistency
D	Prudence	Going concern

2 Marks

29   Fill in three missing words

Prudence is the concept whereby in situations of ...., appropriate ....is exercised in .... transactions in financial records.   **2 Marks**

30   On 30 April 20X1 an engineering company purchases hardware upgrades for all of its computers, at a cost of $24,000. This upgrade will speed up design work and reduce costs. Nobody explains this to the accounts department, and the cost gets written off to computer repairs. Computer equipment is written off over 4 years with a proportional charge in the year of acquisition.

Profit for the year to 30 June 20X1 has been understated by _____   **2 Marks**

31   During the year, a car was traded in for $3,000 against the cost ($10,000) of a new car. The old car had cost $8,000 and had a net book value at the time of trade in of $2,000.

The balance due on the new car was paid in cash and was debited to the cars account. No other entries were made.

What net adjustment is required to the cars cost account?

A   Dr $10,000
B   Dr $3,000
C   Cr $8,000
D   Cr $5,000   **2 Marks**

32   On 31 March 20X9 a machine was sold which cost $20,000 on 1 May 20X5. The profit on disposal was $1,500. The depreciation policy is 20% pa straight line, with a full year being charged in year of acquisition and none in the year of sale. The year end is 31 December.

The sale proceeds were $_____.   **2 Marks**

33   A business buys a machine for $30,000. The depreciation policy for machinery is 15% pa reducing balance. What is the net book value of the machine after two years of use?

$_____.   **2 Marks**

34   Complete the two missing words.

Depreciation is a measure of the cost or revalued amount of the economic .... that have been .... during the period.   **2 Marks**

35   Fill in the missing two words.

An intangible non-current asset is an asset that does not have .... existence. It cannot be ....   **2 Marks**

36 A car was purchased by a florist business in May 20W7 for:

	$
Cost	20,000
Road tax	300
Total	20,300

The business adopts a date of 31 December as its year end.

The car was traded in for a replacement vehicle in August 20X0 at an agreed value of $10,000.

It has been depreciated at 25% per annum on the reducing-balance method, charging a full year's depreciation in the year of purchase and none in the year of sale.

What was the profit or loss on disposal of the vehicle during the year ended December 20X0?

A   Profit: $1,436
B   Profit: $1,562
C   Profit: $3,576
D   Profit: $3,672   **2 Marks**

37 On 1 June 20X9 a machine was sold which cost $10,000 on 31 July 20X5. Sale proceeds were $2,750 and the profit on disposal was $750. The depreciation policy for machinery is straight line with a full year being charged in the year of acquisition and none in the year of sale.

What is the depreciation rate? _____%   **2 Marks**

38 Which of the following statements are correct?

(1)   Capitalised development expenditure must be amortised over a period not exceeding five years.
(2)   Capitalised development costs are shown in the statement of financial position under the heading of Non-current Assets
(3)   If certain criteria are met, research expenditure must be recognised as an intangible asset.

A   2 only
B   2 and 3
C   1 only
D   1 and 3

39 Insert one of the following in each box: receivables, payables, income statement, trading account.

Carriage inward is posted to:

DR [ ]   CR [ ]

Carriage outward is posted to:

DR [ ]   CR [ ]   **2 Marks**

40 A business receives and issues the following invoices and cash receipts and payments. There was no inventory of goods for sale at either the beginning or end of the month.

	Invoice date	Amount	Date paid or received
		$	
Purchases	8.9.X1	100	20.9.X1
	10.9.X1	200	2.10.X1
Sales	12.9.X1	200	25.9.X1
	30.9.X1	300	5.10.X1

Required

(a) The profit earned in September on a cash basis was:

Sales	$
Purchase	$
Profit	$

(b) The profit earned in September on an accruals basis was:

Sales	$	
Purchase	$	
Profit	$	**5 Marks**

41 A trial balance contains the following:

	$
Opening inventory	2,000
Closing inventory	4,000
Purchases	20,000
Purchases returned	400
Carriage inwards	3,000
Prompt payment discounts received	1,600

What is the cost of sales?

A $17,600
B $19,000
C $20,600
D $24,600   **2 Marks**

42 Following the inventory count, a total inventory valuation is reached of $120,357. The auditors find the following additional information:

(i) 370 units of inventory which cost $4.0 have been valued at $0.40 each.

(ii) The inventory count includes damaged goods at their original cost of $2,885. These goods could be repaired at a cost of $921 and sold for $3,600.

(iii) The count includes 440 items at their original cost of $8.50. These are normally sold at $15 but, due to shortages in the market and increased demand, they will now be sold for $18.50 each.

The correct year end inventory figure is:_____   **2 Marks**

43 Which two of the following statements are true?

(i) In times of inflation, FIFO will give you a higher profit than LIFO.
(ii) In times of Inflation LIFO will give you a higher profit than FIFO.
(iii) FIFO matches revenue with up to date costs
(iv) LIFO matches revenue with up to date costs

A (I) and (III)
B (i) and (iv)
C (ii) and (iii)
D (ii) and (iv)

2 Marks

44 These records were kept for a inventory item in May.

May 1 100 units in inventory at $10 each
5 50 units bought at $10 each
12 60 units sold
20 20 units bought at $8 each
29 80 units sold

The value of the inventory at May 31st:

(a) Using FIFO is $_____.
(b) Using LIFO is $_____.

2 Marks

45 Carriage inwards $75,000 has been recorded in the I/S account as an expense. As a result?

A Net profit is understated by $75,000
B Gross profit is overstated by $75,000, net profit is unchanged
C Gross profit is understated by $75,000
D Net profit is overstated by $75,000

2 Marks

46 What does the phrase 'proper cut-off procedures' mean in relation to the sale of goods?

A All orders are processed and invoiced to customers.

B Inventory records correctly record receipts and dispatches of goods for resale.

C Arrangements to ensure that all goods dispatched prior to the cut off point are either invoiced or accrued in the financial statements.

D Having in place arrangements to check invoices prior to dispatch to customers.

2 Marks

47 Net realisable value means? (In relation to the valuation of inventory.)

A The expected selling price of the inventory.

B The expected selling price less disposals costs less, in the case of incomplete items, the cost of completion.

C The replacement cost of the inventory.

D The market price as adjusted for the condition of the inventory item.

2 Marks

48 The following transactions take place during a sales tax quarter:

	$
Sales on credit including sales tax at 17.5%	127,000
Purchases on credit including sales tax	58,000
Credit notes issued including sales tax	3,000
Sales tax incurred on deductible cash expenses	271.50

The amount payable to the tax authorities for the quarter will be $ _____

2 Marks

49 Which of the following is *not* a valid reason for not adding 17.5% sales tax on the goods sold by a business?

A   A business is not registered for sales tax.
B   The customer is not registered for sales tax.
C   The business made sales of exempt products.
D   The business made sales of zero-rated products.

2 Marks

50 In its first period of trading a business has charged sales tax of $12,000 on its credit sales and $2,000 on its cash sales. Sales tax suffered on credit purchases is $3,000 and on cash expenses and purchases is $1,500. The amount owed to the government is $_____.

2 Marks

51 Sales tax is administered by

A   Office of Value Added Taxes
B   The Treasury
C   The tax authorities
D   Commissioner of Indirect Taxes

2 Marks

52 From the information given below you are required:

(a)   To calculate the charge to the income statement for the year ended 30 June 20X6 in respect of rent, rates and insurance.

(b)   To state the amount of accrual or prepayment for rent, rates and insurance as at 30 June 20X6.

The accruals and prepayments as at 30 June 20X5 were as follows.

	$
Rent accrued	2,000
Rates prepaid	1,500
Insurance prepaid	1,800

Payments made during the year ended 30 June 20X6 were as follows.

20X5		$
10 August	Rent, three months to 31 July 20X5	3,000
26 October	Insurance, one year to 31 October 20X6	6,000
2 November	Rates, six months to 31 March 20X6	3,500
12 December	Rent, four months to 30 November 20X5	4,000
20X6		
17 April	Rent, four months to 31 March 20X6	4,000
9 May	Rates, six months to 30 September 20X6	3,500

	(a) *Income statement charge*	(b) *Accrual*	*Prepayment*	
Rent	_____	_____	_____	**2 Marks**
Rates	_____	_____	_____	**2 Marks**
Insurance	_____	_____	_____	**2 Marks**

53 During the year, $3,000 was paid to the electricity board. At the beginning of the year, $1,000 was owed, at the year end, $1,200 was owed.

What is the charge for electricity in the year's income statement?

A $3,000
B $3,200
C $4,000
D $5,200   **2 Marks**

54 A business received or issued the following invoices and paid or received the invoiced amounts on the following dates:

	Invoice date	Invoice amount	Date paid or received
Purchase	2.6.X4	$1,000	26.6.X4
	25.6.X4	$1,500	2.7.X4
Sales	8.6.X4	$2,000	26.6.X4
	29.6.X4	$3,000	7.7.X4

There is no inventory at the beginning or end of June.

What is the difference between the profit for June calculated on a cash basis, and calculated on an accruals basis?

A Nil
B $1,000
C $1,500
D $2,500   **2 Marks**

55 At 1 January 20X1, there was allowance for receivables of $2,000. During the year, $1,000 of debts was written off, and $800 of bad debts were recovered. At 31 December 20X1, it was decided to adjust the allowance for receivables to 10% of receivables which are $30,000.

What is the total bad debt expense for the year?

A $200
B $1,200
C $2,000
D $2,800   **2 Marks**

56 At the beginning of the year, the allowance for receivables was $3,400. At the year-end, the allowance required was $4,000. During the year $2,000 of debts were written off, which includes $400 previously provided for.

What is the charge to income statement for bad debts for the year?

A $6,000
B $4,000
C $2,600
D $2,200   **2 Marks**

57   The cash book has a balance of $1622, while the bank statement shows that the account is overdrawn by $370.

The reconciling items are as follows:

(a)   A bounced cheque from a customer for $125 not posted to the cash book
(b)   Cash of $3500 paid into the bank but not yet credited
(c)   An unposted direct debit of $75
(d)   Unpresented cheques totalling $1721
(e)   Bank charges of $13 not posted

The correct month end cash balance is: $_____.   **2 Marks**

58   A debit entry in the cash book will have which effect on the level of a bank overdraft and a bank balance?

	Bank overdraft	*Bank balance*
A	Increase	Increase
B	Decrease	Decrease
C	Increase	Decrease
D	Decrease	Increase

2 Marks

59   When preparing a bank reconciliation, it is realised that:

(i)   There are unpresented cheques of $3,000.
(ii)   There are unrecorded lodgements of $2,500.
(iii)   Bank charges of $35 have not been recorded in the cash book.
(iv)   A cheque written out to pay a supplier $39 was entered in the cash book as $93.

The necessary adjustment to the cash book is a debit/credit of $_____.   **2 Marks**

60   When preparing a bank reconciliation, it is realised that:

(i)   There are unpresented cheques of $16,000
(ii)   There are unrecorded lodgements of $10,000
(iii)   Bank charges of $134 have not been recorded in the cash book

What adjustment is required to the cash account?

A   Debit $134
B   Credit $134
C   Debit $6,134
D   Credit $6,134   **2 Marks**

61   A company has the following monthly payroll costs:

Net wages paid	13,330
PAYE deducted	4,070
Employee NI deducted	2,600
Employer NI contribution	2,900

The total income statement charge for wages for the month is $_____.   **2 Marks**

62 Gross payroll cost recorded in the income statement is:

A   Gross pay paid to employees plus employers National Insurance contributions and any employers pension contributions.

B   Net pay paid to employees' plus employer's National Insurance contributions and any employer's pension contributions.

C   Gross pay paid to employees plus employer's and employees' National Insurance contributions.

D   Net pay paid to employees plus employer's and employees' National Insurance contributions.

2 Marks

63 The double entry to record PAYE and employees' National Insurance contributions is:

DEBIT   _____

CREDIT   _____

CREDIT   _____   **2 Marks**

64 An employee has a gross monthly salary of $2,000. In September the tax deducted was $400, the employee's national insurance was $120, and the employer's national insurance was $200. What was the charge for salaries in the income statement?

A $1,480
B $1,880
C $2,000
D $2,200   **2 Marks**

65 At the year end the total of balances on the sales ledger is $17,251 and the balance on the receivables control account is $19,158.

The following discrepancies are discovered:

(a)   A purchase ledger offset of $240 has not been posted to the receivables control account.

(b)   The total of one sales ledger account has been overcast by $90

(c)   The March daybook total of $7800 had been posted as $8700

(d)   A bad debt of $325 had been removed from the sales ledger but no entry had been made in the receivables control account.

(e)   A customer balance of $532 had been omitted from the list of balances

The correct sales ledger balance is: $_____.   **2 Marks**

66 When reconciling the payables control account to the list of balances, it was discovered than an invoice received from a supplier for $72 had been recorded in the purchases day book as $27.

What adjustment is necessary to the control account and the list of balances?

	Control account	List of balances
A	Debit $45	Add $45
B	Credit $45	Add $45
C	Debit $45	Subtract $45
D	Credit $45	Subtract $45

2 Marks

67 Which of the following is *not* the purpose of a receivables control account?

A   A sales ledger control account provides a check on the arithmetical accuracy of the personal ledger
B   A sales ledger control account helps to improve separation of duties
C   A sales ledger control account ensures that there are no errors in the personal ledger
D   Control accounts deter fraud   **2 Marks**

68 When reconciling the receivables control account to the list of balances, it was discovered that the sales daybook has been overcast by $100.

What adjustment is necessary to the list of balances?

A   No adjustment
B   Add $100
C   Subtract $100
D   Subtract $200   **2 Marks**

69 An invoice for $18 received from a supplier is recorded as $81 in the purchases day book. When this error is corrected, it will affect:

A   An account in the purchase ledger only
B   Accounts in the nominal ledger only
C   An account in the purchase ledger and accounts in the nominal ledger
D   No accounts   **2 Marks**

70 A business has prepared its draft income statement which shows gross profit of $5,500 and net profit of $3,000. It is then realised that an invoice for $250 relating to cost of sales has been treated as an administration expense by mistake.

The correction of this error will **increase/decrease** gross profit by $_____ and **increase/decrease** net profit by $_____.   **2 Marks**

71 When a trial balance was prepared, two ledger accounts were omitted.

Discounts received $1,500
Discounts allowed $1,000

The total of debit balances exceeds/falls below the total of credit balances by $_____.   **2 Marks**

72 The sales day book has been undercast by $50, and an invoice for $20 has been entered into the sales day book twice.

The necessary adjustment to the receivables control account is $_____ debit/credit.   **2 Marks**

73   When a trial balance was prepared, a suspense account was opened. It was discovered that the only error that had been made was to record $350 of discounts received on the wrong side of the trial balance.

What is the journal to correct this error?

A	Dr	Discounts received	$350
	Cr	Suspense	$350
B	Dr	Suspense	$350
	Cr	Discounts received	$350
C	Dr	Discounts received	$700
	Cr	Suspense	$700
D	Dr	Suspense	$700
	Cr	Discounts received	$700	2 Marks

74   Materials used to repair some machinery have been treated as purchases in the draft account. Correcting this error will have what effect on gross profit and net assets?

	Gross profit	Net assets
A	Increase	No change
B	Increase	Increase
C	Decrease	Decrease
D	No change	Increase

2 Marks

75   When a trial balance was prepared, two ledger accounts were omitted:

Discounts received $6,150
Discounts allowed $7,500

To make a trial balance balance, a suspense account was opened.

What was the balance on the suspense account?

A   Debit $1,350
B   Credit $1,350
C   Debit $13,650
D   Credit $13,650

2 Marks

76   A reduction in the cost of goods resulting from the nature of the trading transaction is a

A   Bad debt
B   Cash discount
C   Impairment
D   Trade discount

2 Marks

77   The following trial balance is extracted at 31 December 20X1:

	DR	CR
Sales		321,726
Purchases	202,419	
Carriage inwards	376	
Carriage outwards	729	
Wages and salaries	54,210	
Rent and rates	12,466	
Heat and light	1,757	
Inventory at 1 January 20X1	14,310	
Drawings	28,500	
Receivables	49,633	
Payables		32,792
Bank		3,295
Sundry expenses	18,526	
Cash	877	
Capital		28,990
	386,803	386,803

Closing inventory is 15,327

(a)   Gross profit for the year is $ _____   **2 Marks**

(b)   Net profit for the year is $ _____   **2 Marks**

(c)   Net assets are $ _____   **2 Marks**

78   Which of these transactions would *not* increase a company's retained earnings for the year?

A   Revaluation of a freehold factory from $140,000 to $250,000.

B   Receipt of $5,000 from a receivable previously written off.

C   Receive discounts of $1,000 from a supplier.

D   Sell for $6,000 a car which cost $10,000 and has been depreciated by $4,500.   **2 Marks**

79   A company has profit before tax of $140,000. The tax charge for the year is $25,000 and $15,000 is to be transferred to a non-current asset reserve. A final dividend of 5c per ordinary share is proposed. In the year these dividends were paid:

	$
Last year's final dividend on 375,000 25c ordinary shares	15,000
This year's interim dividend on 375,000 25c ordinary shares	10,000
This year's interim dividend on 100,000 6% preference shares	3,000

The retained earnings for the year is $_____.   **2 Marks**

80   When preparing financial statements in periods of inflation, directors

A   Must reduce asset values

B   Must increase asset values

C   Must reduce salaries

D   Need make no adjustments   **2 Marks**

81 A particular source of finance has the following characteristics: a fixed return, a fixed repayment date, it is secured and the return is classified as an expense.

Is the source of finance

A   Ordinary share
B   Hire purchase
C   Loan stock
D   Preference share   **2 Marks**

82 At 31 December 20X1, a business had net assets of $10,000. At 31 December 20X2 net assets had risen to $12,500. Profit for the year was $8,000 and no new capital was introduced. How much were drawings in the period.

A $2,500
B $3,000
C $5,500
D $10,500   **2 Marks**

83 At 1 January 20X4 a business had net assets of $13,000. By 31 December 20X4 it had:

	$
Buildings	4,000
Furniture	2,000
Bank overdraft	1,500
Receivables	3,500
Payables	2,000
Proprietors capital	6,000

During the year the proprietor had introduced $1,000 of new capital and had drawings of $800. The profit (loss) for the year is _____   **2 Marks**

84 On 30 April 20X1 part of a company's inventory was destroyed by fire.

The following information is available:

- Inventory at 1 April 20X1 $99,600
- Purchases for April 20X1 $177,200
- Sales for April 20X1 $260,000
- Inventory at 30 April 20X1 – undamaged items $64,000
- Standard gross profit percentage on sales 30%

Based on this information, the cost of the inventory destroyed is _____   **2 Marks**

85 Hamilton runs a bicycle repair shop and keeps no accounting records. All of his sales are for cash, which he says is all banked. He has a few unpaid bills and he shows you a copy of last year's statement of financial position, which shows net assets of 8537. He withdraws $100 per week for living expenses.

You arrive at the following figures for the year ended 31.12.X1

Van:

Cost	3,000
Depreciation	(1,800)
	1200
Inventory	125
Cash at bank	8,504
Cash on hand	127
Payables	1,035

His net profit for the year is $_____   **2 Marks**

86   At 1 January 20X1 payables were owed $10,000, by 31 December 20X1 they were owed $8,000. In the year, receivables and payables contras were $3,500, and $350 of debit balances were transferred to receivables, credit purchases were $60,000 and $2,500 of discounts were received.

What was paid to suppliers during the year?

A $55,650
B $56,000
C $56,350
D $58,000   2 Marks

07   During the year, all sales were made at a gross profit margin of 10%. Sales were $25,000, purchases were $22,000 and closing inventory was $5,000.

Opening inventory was $_____.   2 Marks

88   Sales for the year are 525,329 and the normal mark-up on cost is 25%. Opening Inventory was 77,505 and closing inventory is 79,350.

Purchases are _____   2 Marks

89   At 31 March 20X8, a business had:

Motor cars	6,000
Inventory	1,500
Receivables	900
Accrued electricity expense	150
Rent prepaid	600

At 31 March 20X9, it had:

Motor cars	7,500
Inventory	300
Receivables	150
Payables	1,800
Accrued electricity expense	300
Rent prepaid	750

The owner has drawn $3,000 in cash over the year.

What is the profit or loss?

A   Loss $750
B   Profit $750
C   Loss $2,250
D   Profit $2,250   2 Marks

90   A business has opening inventory $30,000, achieves a mark up of 25% on sales, sales totalled $1,000,000, purchases were $840,000. Calculate closing inventory.

A $30,000
B $40,000
C $120,000
D $70,000   2 Marks

91 Opening inventory of raw materials was $29,000, closing inventory was $31,500, purchases were $128,000, purchase returns were $8,500. What was cost of sales?

A $128,000
B $117,000
C $119,500
D $122,000   2 Marks

92 A business achieves a margin of 25% on sales. Opening inventory was $36,000, closing inventory was $56,000 and purchases totalled $800,000. Calculate the sales for the period.

A $773,333
B $725,000
C $826,666
D $800,000   2 Marks

93 A company has a gross profit margin of 10% and an asset turnover of 3 times a year.

What is the return on capital employed?

A   3.33%
B   7%
C   13%
D   30%   2 Marks

94 A company has sales of $420,000 spread evenly over the year. All sales are on credit with a trade receivables collection period of 2 months. Cost of sales are $240,000 and the inventory turnover period is 1 month. The company gets on average 45 days credit from its suppliers.

The company's working capital (excluding cash) is $_____.

The cash cycle is _____ months.   2 Marks

95 Working capital is?

A   Current assets – inventory – current liabilities
B   Current assets – current liabilities
C   Total assets – total liabilities
D   Liquid current assets – current liabilities   2 Marks

96 The annual sales of a company are $47,000 including sales tax at 17.5%. Half of the sales are on credit terms; half are cash sales. The receivables are $4,700.

What is the trade receivables collection period (to the nearest day)?

A   37 days
B   43 days
C   73 days
D   86 days   2 Marks

97 If sales were $51,000, and cost of sales was $42,500, what was the gross profit percentage?

A   16.67%
B   20%
C   83.333%
D   120%   2 Marks

98   Which of the following costs would **not** be shown as a factory overhead in a manufacturing account?

A   The cost of insurance on a factory
B   The cost of extension to a factory
C   The cost of depreciation on a factory
D   The cost of rent on a factory   **2 Marks**

99   Which of the following costs would be included in the calculation of prime cost in a manufacturing account?

A   Factory rent
B   Office wages
C   Direct production wages
D   Depreciation and machinery   **2 Marks**

100   The following information relates to transactions for the year ended 31 December 20X1.

	$'000
Depreciation	1,320
Increase in inventory	555
Cash paid to employees	4,230
Decease in receivables	420
Decrease in payables	585
Net profit before tax	3,555

Net cash flow from operating activities is $_____

101   A business had net cash flow from operating activities of $80,000, and these results:

	$
Operating profit	23,000
Depreciation	4,000
Loss on sale of non-current assets	22,000
Decrease in inventory	13,000
Increase in payables	10,000

What was the change in receivables?

A   No change
B   Decrease of $8,000
C   Increase of $18,000
D   Decrease of $5,000   **2 Marks**

102   Which two of the following would cause net cash flow from operating activities in the statement of cash flows to be bigger than operating profit in the income statement.

(i)   An increase in inventories of raw materials
(ii)   A decrease in inventories of finished goods
(iii) A profit on the sale of a non-current asset
(iv)   A loss on the sale of a non-current asset   **2 Marks**

103 Barry Co has the following payments and receipts during its accounting period. Issue of shares $1,030,000, debenture repaid $400,000, share premium received $460,000, proceeds of a rights issue $630,000, interest paid $115,000. Calculate the 'financing' cash flow figure for its statement of cash flows.

A $1,720,000
B $1,090,000
C $1,490,000
D $1,260,000   **2 Marks**

104 When comparing two statements of financial position you notice that:

(i) Last year the company had included in current assets investments of $5,000. This year there are no investments in current assets.

(ii) Last year the company had an overdraft of $4,000, this year the overdraft is $2,000.

In the statement of cash flows, the change in cash would be:

A Increase $2,000
B Decrease $2,000
C Increase $3,000
D Decrease $3,000   **2 Marks**

105 At 1 January 20X4 a club had $500 of subscriptions received in advance and 10 members still owed $20 each for their year's subscription. At 31 December $600 had been received in advance for next year and $180 was owed by members. During the year $1,200 was received from members.

The amount credited to the income and expenditure account for the year to 31.12.X4 was:

A $480
B $1,080
C $1,200
D $1,920   **2 Marks**

106 At the beginning of the year, a club had subscriptions in arrears of $50 and subscriptions received in advance of $80. At the end of the year, subscriptions in arrears were $100, and subscriptions received in advance were $60. Subscriptions received in the year were $2,060.

(a) The figure for subscriptions in an income and expenditure account would be $_____.

(b) The figure for subscriptions in a receipts and payments record would be $_____.   **2 Marks**

107 Write the full names of the following accounting bodies.

(i) FRC _____
(ii) FRRP _____
(iii) ASB _____   **2 Marks**

108 Who issues Financial Reporting Standards?

A The Auditing Practices Board
B The Stock Exchange
C The Accounting Standards Board
D CIMA   **2 Marks**

109   Which of the following is not a member of the Consultative Committee of Accounting Bodies (CCAB)?

A   The Chartered Institute of Management Accountants
B   The Chartered Association of Certified Accountants
C   The Institutes of Chartered Accountants in England, Wales, Scotland and Ireland
D   The Association of Accounting Technicians   2 Marks

110   Insert the missing two words

The International Accounting Standards Committee has been replaced by the ....
.... Accounting Standards ....   2 Marks

111   The role of the Financial Reporting Council is to?

A   Oversee the standard setting and regulatory process
B   Formulate accounting standards
C   Review defective accounts
D   Control the accountancy profession   2 Marks

112   Auditing Standards and Guidelines are issued by

A   Audit Standards Board
B   The Audit Practices Board
C   The Audit Standards and Guidelines Committee
D   The Audit Practices Committee.   2 Marks

113   Which two of the following are detect controls?

(i)   Bank reconciliations
(ii)   Reconciliation of asset register to physical assets
(iii) Matching invoices to goods received notes prior to payment
(iv)   Matching wages calculations to clock cards prior to payment   2 Marks

114   Which is the single most important attribute of an auditor (external or internal)?

A   Professional skills and training
B   Computer literacy
C   Independence
D   Ability to work closely with management   2 Marks

115   An internal auditor identifies an internal control weakness in an accounting system. What action should now be taken?

A   Consider the effect of the weakness and identify counter controls
B   Report to management
C   Instruct the operators of the system to change the procedures in use
D   Report it to the police   2 Marks

116   The primary reason for an external audit is to:

A   Give an opinion on the financial statements
B   Detect any material errors or frauds
C   Supplement the work of internal audit
D   Confirm the financial viability and adaptability of the company   2 Marks

117   Fair presentation is determined by reference to:

    A   Compliance with company law
    B   Compliance with accounting standards
    C   Compliance with generally accepted accounting practice
    D   The meaning of the word 'fair'.   **2 Marks**

118   Who appoints external auditors?

    A   Directors
    B   Registrar of Companies
    C   Finance director
    D   Shareholders   **2 Marks**

119   Which of the following statements is correct?

    A   External auditors report to the directors
    B   External auditors are appointed by the directors
    C   External auditors are required to give a report to shareholders
    D   External auditors correct only material errors in financial statements   **2 Marks**

120   What is an audit trail in a computerised accounting system?

    A   A list of all the transactions in a period
    B   A list of all the transactions in a ledger account in a period
    C   A list of all the items checked by the auditor
    D   A list of special transactions printed for the auditor to examine   **2 Marks**

121   Which of the following is *not* an activity which internal auditors would normally carry out?

    A   Fraud investigations
    B   Value for money studies
    C   Controls testing
    D   The statutory audit   **2 Marks**

122   Internal control includes 'detect' controls and 'prevent' controls. Which of the following is a detect control?

    A   Installation of security cameras
    B   Matching purchase invoices with goods received notes
    C   Preparing bank reconciliations
    D   Matching sales invoices with delivery notes   **2 Marks**

123   What do you understand by the term 'management fraud'?

    A   Abuse of company credit cards
    B   Fraud designed to improve the company's position or performance
    C   Using creative accounting
    D   Theft by managers   **2 Marks**

124   What controls are concerned with achieving the objectives of the organisation and implementing policies?

    A   Accounting controls
    B   Financial controls
    C   Administrative controls
    D   Detect controls   **2 Marks**

125 Fill in the two missing words.

An external audit is an ………………………… examination of, and expression of ………………………… on the financial statements of an enterprise.

2 Marks

Answer bank

1   Shareholders
    Potential investors
    Employees
    Providers of finance
    Financial analysts
    Government departments
    Trade unions
    Payables

2   B

3   Management accounting is the preparation of accounting reports for internal use.

4   A   This is the actual objective of accounting.

5

Assets		Capital		Liabilities
7,000	=	5,500	+	1,500

6   B

7   Assets = Capital + Liabilities

    159,500 = 158,500 + 1,000
    Assets
    Bank = 155,000 capital introduced - 80,000 vehicles - 500 rent + 10,000 sales = 84,500
    Vehicles = 80,000 bank - 5,000 van - 5,000 vehicles sold = 70,000
    Van = 5,000 transfer from vehicles

    Capital
    Capital = 155,000 capital introduced
    Profit = (10,000 sales - 5,000 cost of sales) - 500 rent - 1,000 repairs = 3,500

    Liabilities
    Repair bills not yet paid = 1,000

8   Capital expenditure: (a), (d)
    Revenue expenditure: (b), (c), (e), (f) (Note that the value of the transactions is irrelevant.)

9   A   Correct.
    B   Incorrect, this is repairs not improvement
    C   Incorrect, reoccurrence is not important
    D   Incorrect, the fact that it is such a small amount is more likely to justify its treatment as a revenue item

10 C   Correct, it is likely to be treated as capital expenditure.
    A   This is printing and stationery, so it is revenue expenditure.
    B   This is a repair and renewal expense so it would be likely to be treated as a revenue item.
    D   Incorrect, these are unlikely to be sufficiently expensive to warrant treatment as capital expenditure.

11 Return is a reward for investment in a business.

12 The sales day book lists all invoices sent to customers.
    The purchases day book lists all invoices received from suppliers.
    The sales returns day book lists all credit notes sent to customers.
    The purchases returns day book lists all credit notes received from suppliers.

13   C

14   Source documents are recorded in day books. The totals of day books are posted by double entry to ledger accounts in the nominal ledger.

Individual invoice details in the day books are posted by single entry to accounts in the personal ledgers.

15 $30.50

16   (a)   DR Payables   CR Purchases
         (b)   DR Cash   CR Payables

17   D

18   The sales and purchases ledgers are not part of the double entry system. They are memorandum accounts only.

19   A   The total of the cash paid column should be credited to the cash control account.

20   C is correct. The clerk has done two credits of $250, and no debit, so credits will exceed debits by $500.

21   Purchases should be a debit balance so credits will exceed debits by $6,000.

22   Gross profit is $6,800.

		$	$
Sales			12,500
Less cost of sales			
Opening inventory		400	
Purchases		6,000	
Carriage inwards		200	
		6,600	
Closing inventory $(1,100 – 200)		(900)	
			(5,700)
Gross profit			6,800

23   Accruals
         Consistency
         Prudence

24   D   Making an allowance for receivables and bad debts follows the prudence concept, ie recognising a potential loss.

25   The accruals basis of accounting requires that, in computing profit, amounts are included in the accounts in the period when they are earned or incurred, not received or paid.

26   C   Where there is tension between the concepts of accruals and prudence a neutral approach must be adopted that ensures a fair presentation.

27   The double entry system of bookkeeping is based on the concept of duality.

28   C

29   Prudence is the concept whereby in situations of uncertainty, appropriate caution is exercised in recognising transactions in financial records.

30   Profit has been understated by $23,000.

Charge put through accounts in error	24,000
Depreciation charge ($24,000 \times 25\% \times 2/12$)	(1,000)
Total understated	23,000

31 D is correct.

	$	$
Existing debit in cars account (10,000 – 3,000)	7,000	
Transfer proceeds to disposals account	3,000	3,000
Cost of new car	10,000	
Transfer cost of car sold to disposal account		(8,000)
∴ Net adjustment		(5,000)

32 Sales proceeds were $5,500.

31.7.X5

	$
Cost	20,000
Depreciation y/e 31.12.X5 to y/e 31.12.X8	16,000
NBV at date of sale	4,000
Profit on disposal	1,500
⇒ Sale proceeds	5,500

33 $21,675

	$
Cost	30,000
1st year depreciation – 15%	(4,500)
Net book value	25,500
2nd year depreciation – 15%	3,825
Net book value	21,675

34 IAS 16 defines depreciation as a measure of the cost or revalued amount of the economic benefits that have been consumed during the period.

35 An intangible non-current asset is an asset that does not have physical existence. It cannot be touched.

36 B

	$
Cost	20,000
20W7 Depreciation	(5,000)
	15,000
20W8 Depreciation	(3,750)
	11,250
20W9 Depreciation	(2,812)
	8,438
20X0 Part exchange	10,000
Profit	(1,562)

37 20%

The asset has been depreciated for 4 years (X5, X6, X7 and X8).

	$
Sales proceeds	2,750
Profit on disposal	(750)
Net book value at disposal	2,000
Cost	10,000
Depreciation to date	8,000

ie $2,000 pa which is 20% of $10,000.

38 A Research expenditure must be charged to the income statement.

39 DR Trading account   CR   Payables
      DR Income statement   CR   Payables

40 (a) The profit earned in September on a cash basis was:

	$
Sales	200
Purchases	(100)
Profit	100

      (b) The profit earned in September on an accruals basis was:

	$
Sales	500
Purchases	(300)
Profit	200

41 C

	$
Purchases	20,000
Less purchase returns	(400)
	19,600
Add carriage inwards	3,000
Add opening inventory	2,000
Less closing inventory	(4,000)
Cost of sales	20,600

42 $121,483 (120,357 + (370 × $3.60) − 2,885 + 2,679)

43 B. (i) and (iv) are correct.

Under LIFO, inventory is the oldest receipts, so cost of sales is at current (higher) prices which reduces profit.

44 FIFO is $260, LIFO is $300.

Under FIFO

	Units		Value $
May 1	100	@ $10	1,000
May 5	50	@ $10	500
Balance	150	@ $10	1,500
May 12	(60)	@ $10	(600)
Balance	90	@ $10	900
May 20	20	@ $8	160
Balance	110	@ $8	1,060
May 29	(80)	@ $10	(800)
	30		260

Under LIFO

	Units		Value $
May 1	100	@ $10	1,000
May 5	50	@ $10	500
Balance	150	@ $10	1,500
May 12	(60)	@ $10	(600)
Balance	90	@ $10	900
May 20	20	@ $8	160
Balance	110	@ $8	1,060
May 29	(20)	@ $8	(160)
	(60)	@ $10	(600)
	30		300

45   B   Correct, carriage inwards should be treated as part of the cost of purchases in the trading account.

46   C   Correct. Under the accruals concept, all dispatches in a period must be invoiced or accrued so they can be matched with costs of sale. Goods dispatched must be deducted from inventory records.

     A   This is a completeness control.

     B   This is an accuracy control.

     D   Again, this is an accuracy control.

47   B   Correct.
     A   Incorrect.
     C   Incorrect.
     D   Incorrect.

48 $9,558.28

49   B is correct.

The others are all valid reasons for not adding sales tax on sales invoices.

50 $9,500

SALES TAX PAYABLE

	$		$
Payables	3,000	Receivables	12,000
Cash	1,500	Cash	2,000
C/d	9,500		
	14,000		14,000
		B/d	9,500

51   C   Sales tax is administered by the tax authorities.

52   (a)   *Rent for the year ending 30 June 20X6*

	$
1 July 20X5 to 31 July 20X5 = $3,000/3	1,000
1 August 20X5 to 30 November 20X5	4,000
1 December 20X5 to 31 March 20X6	4,000
Accrued, 1 April 20X6 to 30 June 20X6 = 3/4 × $4,000	3,000
Charge to income statement for year ending 30 June 20X6	12,000

Rates for the year ending 30 June 20X6

	$	$
Rates prepaid last year, relating to this year		1,500
1 October 20X5 to 31 March 20X6		3,500
1 April 20X6 to 30 September 20X6	3,500	
Less prepaid July to September (3/6)	1,750	
April to June 20X6		1,750
Charge to income statement for year ending 30 June 20X6		6,750

Insurance for the year ending 30 June 20X6

	$	$
Insurance prepaid last year, relating to this year		1,800
1 November 20X5 to 31 October 20X6	6,000	
Less prepaid July to October (4/12)	2,000	
		4,000
Charge to income statement for year ending 30 June 20X6		5,800

(b)   The accrual or prepayment for each expense can be summarised from the workings in part (a).

As at 30 June 20X6	$
Rent accrued	3,000
Rates prepaid	1,750
Insurance prepaid	2,000

53   B

ELECTRICITY EXPENSE ACCOUNT

	$		$
Cash	3,000	B/d	1,000
C/d	1,200	I/S	3,200
	4,200		4,200
		B/d	1,200

54   C   On a cash basis

	$
Sales	2,000
Purchases	1,000
Profit	1,000

On an accruals basis

	$
Sales	5,000
Purchases	2,500
Profit	2,500

Thus, the difference is $1,500.

55   B

ALLOWANCE

	$		$
		B/d	2,000
C/d	3,000	Bad debts expense	1,000
	3,000		3,000

BAD DEBTS EXPENSE

	$		$
Receivables (write off)	1,000	Cash (write-offs recovered)	800
Increase in allowance	1,000	I/S	1,200
	2,000		2,000

56   C

Allowance

		3,400	b/d
Write off	400		
C/d	4,000	1,000	Expense
	4,400	4,400	

Bad debts expense

Allowance increase	1,000		
Receivables W/O	1,600	2,600	I/S
	2,600	2,600	

57 $1,409

58   D is correct.

When cash is received by a business a debit entry is made in the cash book. A receipt of cash decreases an overdraft and increases a bank balance.

59   Debit $19.

Unpresented cheques and increased lodgements are timing differences so no adjustments is necessary.

The bank charges need a credit to cash of $35.

The transposition errors needs a debit to cash $54, ie a net debit of $19.

60   B   The only adjustment that should be made to the cash account is to record the bank charges. The cheques and lodgements will already have been recorded in the cash account.

61 $22,900

62   A.

63   Debit   Wages control account (total deductions)
        Credit   PAYE control account (PAYE)
        Credit   NIC control account (NIC)

64   D   The charge for the salary in the income statement is the gross salary plus the employer's national insurance contribution. This is $2,000 plus $200 respectively, a total of $2,200.

65 $17,693

66   B.   This affects both the total which was posted to the control account and the individual posting to the purchase ledger.

67 C

68 A   Remember, daybook totals are posted to the control account. Individual invoices are posted to the individual accounts, so an error in a total does not affect the list of balances.

69 C is correct. This error affects the total posted to the purchases account and the payables accounts in the nominal ledger, and it affects the amount posted to the suppliers account in the purchase ledger.

70 Decrease gross profit by $250

No effect on net profit.

This $250 must be 'moved up' to the trading account. This reduces gross profit and has no effect on net profit.

71 We have 'missed' income (and thus a credit balance) of $1,500 and an expense (and thus a debit balance) of $1,000. Thus debit balances will exceed credit balances by $500.

72 Debit $30.

For the undercast	debit $50
For the invoice entered invoice	credit $20
A net debit of	$30

73 D is correct.

Discounts received are income and thus, a credit balance. Recording them as a debit will have made debits in the trial balance exceed credits by $700, ie the suspense account balance is a credit of $700. So the correction is debit suspense $700, and credit discounts received $700.

74 A is correct.

The correction will increase expenses and reduce purchases. Thus gross profit will increase and net assets not change.

75 A

Suspense account

B/d	1,350		
Discounts received	6,150	7,500	Discounts allowed
	7,500	7,500	

76 D   A reduction in the cost of goods resulting from the nature of the trading transaction is a trade discount.

77 (a) $119,948
     (b) $29,260
     (c) $29,750

78 A.

'Profit' on revaluation must be credited to a revaluation reserve, not to retained earnings for the year.

79 $115,000

	$
Profit before tax	140,000
Tax	(25,000)
Retained earnings for the year	115,000

Remember that dividends and transfers to reserves are part of the SOCIE.

80 D

81 C   Loan stock. The other items do not fit the criteria in the question.

82 C.

$P = I + D - C$

$8,000 = 2,500 + D - 0$

$\Rightarrow D = \$5,500$

83 (7,200)

Net assets at 31.12X4 = $4,000 + $2,000 − $1,500 + $3,500 − $2,000 = $6,000 (which is of course equal to capital)

So, the decrease in net assets is $7,000.

$P = I + D - C$

$P = -\$7,000 + \$800 - \$1,000$

$P = -\$7,200$

ie, a loss of $7,200

84

	$
Theoretical gross profit 30% x $260,000	78,000
Actual gross profit:	
$260,000 − $99600 − $177,200 + $64,000	47,200
Shortfall – missing inventory	30,800

85 This is very easy to work out using the business equation ($P = I + D - Ci$).

Net assets for the current year	8,921
Less net assets last year	(8,537)
Increase in net assets (capital)	384
Add drawings	5,200
Less capital introduced	–
Profit for the year	5,584

86 C is correct.

PAYABLES CONTROL ACCOUNT

	$		$
Contra	3,500	B/d	10,000
Discounts received	2,500	Transfers to receivables	350
Cash (balance)	56,350	Purchases	60,000
C/d	8,000		
	70,350		70,350

87 Opening inventory was $5,500.

	$	$
Sales (100%)		25,000
Opening inventory (balance)	5,500	
Purchases	22,000	
Less closing inventory	(5,000)	
Cost of sales (25,000 − 2,500) or 90%		(22,500)
Gross profit (10%)		2,500

88 Purchases are 422,108

Cost of sales = 525,329 × 4/5 =	420,263
Less opening inventory	(77,505)
Add closing inventory	79,350
	422,108

89 B

	$
Net assets 31/12/X1	
6,000 + 1,500 + 900 − 150 + 600	8,850
Net assets 31/12/X2	
7,500 + 300 + 150 − 1,800 − 300 + 750	6,600
Decrease in net assets	2,250

> From the business equation
> Change in net assets = Capital + profit − drawings

−2,250 =	Profit − drawings ($3,000)
−2,250 + 3,000 =	Profit
750 =	Profit

90 D

	$	%
Opening inventory	30,000	
Purchases	840,000	
	870,000	
Closing inventory	(70,000)	
Cost of sales	800,000	100
Gross profit/mark up	200,000	25
Sales	1,000,000	125

Take care you correctly interpret whether you are dealing with gross profit on sales or gross profit on cost.

A   This is opening inventory.

B   This is the difference between cost of sales and purchases ignoring inventory changes.

C   You have incorrectly applied the mark up to sales.

91 B   Correct, $29,000 + $128,000 − $8,500 − $31,500 = $117,000.

A   Incorrect, returns and inventory changes must be allowed for.

C   Incorrect, changes in inventory levels must be allowed for.

D   Incorrect, you have transposed opening and closing inventories.

92 A

	$	%
Opening inventory	36,000	
Purchases	600,000	
	636,000	
Closing inventory	(56,000)	
Cost of sales	580,000	75
Gross profit	193,333	25
Sales	773,333	100

Take care you correctly interpret whether you are dealing with gross profit on sales or gross profit on cost.

B   Incorrect, you have applied the 25% margin to cost of sales.

C   Incorrect because you have transposed the inventory figures in the calculation of cost of sales.

D   Incorrect you have applied a mark up to purchases without the inventory adjustment, ie $600,000 ÷ 75%

93 D is correct.

ROCE = Profit margin × Asset turnover

30% = 10% × 3

94 The company's working capital (excluding cash) is $60,000.

The cash cycle is one and a half months.

	$
Inventories ($1/12$ × $240,000)	20,000
Receivables ($2/12$ × $420,000)	70,000
Less payables ($1.5/12$ × $240,000)	(30,000)
Working capital	60,000

Cash cycle is 1 + 2 − 1.5 = 1.5 months.

95 B Correct. Current assets are normally inventory, receivables, bank. Current liabilities are normally payables, overdraft.

96 C $\dfrac{\text{Receivables including Sales tax}}{\text{Credit sales including Sales tax}} = \dfrac{\$4,700}{\$23,500} \times 365 \text{ days} = 73 \text{ days}$

97 A Gross profit is $51,000 − $42,500 = $8,500, which is 16.67% of $51,000.

90 B The cost of the extension is capital expenditure, which will be shown in non-current assets in the statement of financial position.

99 C Prime cost includes only direct materials and direct production wages. Factory rent and machinery depreciation are factory overheads, so will be deducted before aiming at factory cost of finished goods. Office wages will go to the income statement.

100

	$'000	$'000
Net profit before taxation		3,555
Adjustment for depreciation		1,320
Changes in working capital:		
Increase in inventory	(555)	
Decrease in receivables	420	
Decrease in payables	(585)	(720)
Net cash flow from operating activities		4,155

101 B

	$
Operating profit	23,000
Add depreciation	4,000
Add loss on sale of non-current assets	22,000
Add decrease in inventory	13,000
Add increase in payables	10,000
	72,000
Total cash inflow	80,000
Thus change in receivables produced cash inflow of	8,000

∴ a decrease in receivables

102 (ii) and (iv) are added to operating profit to get cash flow from operating activities.

103 A Correct. $1,030,000 + $460,000 + $630,000 − $400,000 = $1,720,000

B Incorrect, you have not included the rights issue.

C Incorrect, you have included interest paid which is reported under 'returns on investment and servicing finance'.

D Incorrect, you have not included the share premium received.

104 A The reduction in the overdraft is an increase in cash of $2,000.

The reduction in short term investments (of $5,000) would be included in movement in liquid resources (not cash!)

105 B $1,080.

SUBSCRIPTIONS ACCOUNT

	$		$
Arrears b/f	200	Prepaids b/f	500
Income and expenditure a/c (balance)	1,080	Bank/cash	1,200
Prepaid c/f	600	Arrears c/f	180
	1,880		1,880

106

SUBSCRIPTIONS ACCOUNT

	$		$
Arrears b/f	50	Prepaid b/f	80
Income and expenditure a/c (bal)	2,130	Cash	2,060
Prepaid c/f	60	Arrears c/f	100
	2,240		2,240

The figure for subscriptions in an income and expenditure account would be $2,130.

The figure for subscriptions in a receipts and payments account would be $2,060.

107 (i)   Financial Reporting Council
(ii) Financial Reporting Review Panel
(iii) Accounting Standards Board

108 C The Accounting Standards Board
D CIMA – not really!

109 D Correct. Not a member, although the sponsoring bodies of AAT are.
A A member of CCAB.
B A member of CCAB.
C Members of CCAB.

110 The International Accounting Standards Committee has been replaced by the International Accounting Standards Board.

111 A This is correct, the FRC also raises funds and controls the strategic direction of its subsidiary bodies such as the Accounting Standards Board.

B This is the role of the Accounting Standards Board.

C This is the role of the Financial Reporting Review Panel.

D Each professional body is essentially self regulatory. The only avenue for consultation is via the Consultative Committee of Accountancy Bodies.

112   B   Auditing Standards and Guidelines are issued by the Auditing Practice Board (APB).

113   (i) and (ii) are detect controls.
(iii) and (iv) are prevent controls.

114   C   Correct. Unless the auditor is independent from the company, the work or reports will lack credibility in the eyes of users.

       A   This is an important attribute.

       B   This is vital and is developed by adequate training and appropriate experience.

       D   Good relations with management help the audit go smoothly. But independence is key.

115   A   Correct. The impact of the weakness upon control risk should be evaluated, there may be an effective counter control which could mitigate the effects of the weakness.

       B   This should not be done until the facts are checked and cost effective solutions devised.

       C   The auditor should not enforce system changes, this is the role of management on receipt of recommendations from the auditors.

       D   Not valid, not a practical approach!

116   A

117   B

118   D   External auditors are appointed by the shareholders

119   C   This is the Companies Act requirement.

120   D

121   D   Correct, the responsibility rests with the external auditors (although they do rely on internal audit to carry out some of the work at times).

       A   Often in conjunction with the external auditors or a regulatory body.

       B   Studies of efficiency, economy and effectiveness of operations are commonly carried out.

       C   Verifying and suggesting improvements to controls is a key task for internal audit.

122   C

123   B   Correct. Usually this is a characteristic, the fraud is often not performed for personal gain.
       A   This is an example of a type of fraud.
       C   Not all creative accounting devices are necessarily fraudulent.
       D   Management fraud can be simply the theft of assets, but usually it is more complex.

124   C   Administrative controls are concerned with achieving the objectives of the organisation and implementing policies.

125   An external audit is an independent examination of, and expression of, opinion on the financial statements of an enterprise.

Index

Review Form – Paper C02 Fundamentals of Financial Accounting

Please help us to ensure that the CIMA learning materials we produce remain as accurate and user-friendly as possible. We cannot promise to answer every submission we receive, but we do promise that it will be read and taken into account when we up-date this Study Text.

Name: _____ Address: _____

_____

_____

How have you used this Interactive Text?
(Tick one box only)

- [ ] Home study (book only)
- [ ] On a course: college _____
- [ ] With 'correspondence' package
- [ ] Other _____

Why did you decide to purchase this Interactive Text? (Tick one box only)

- [ ] Have used BPP Texts in the past
- [ ] Recommendation by friend/colleague
- [ ] Recommendation by a lecturer at college
- [ ] Saw information on BPP website
- [ ] Saw advertising
- [ ] Other _____

During the past six months do you recall seeing/receiving any of the following?
(Tick as many boxes as are relevant)

- [ ] Our advertisement in Financial Management
- [ ] Our advertisement in PQ
- [ ] Our brochure with a letter through the post
- [ ] Our website www.bpp.com

Which (if any) aspects of our advertising do you find useful?
(Tick as many boxes as are relevant)

- [ ] Prices and publication dates of new editions
- [ ] Information on Text content
- [ ] Facility to order books off-the-page
- [ ] None of the above

Which BPP products have you used?

- [x] Text
- [ ] Kit
- [ ] Passcard
- [ ] Home Study Package
- [ ] Interactive Passcard
- [ ] i-Pass

Your ratings, comments and suggestions would be appreciated on the following areas.

	Very useful	Useful	Not useful
Introductory section (Key study steps, personal study)	[ ]	[ ]	[ ]
Chapter introductions	[ ]	[ ]	[ ]
Key terms	[ ]	[ ]	[ ]
Quality of explanations	[ ]	[ ]	[ ]
Case studies and other examples	[ ]	[ ]	[ ]
Assessment focus points	[ ]	[ ]	[ ]
Questions and answers in each chapter	[ ]	[ ]	[ ]
Fast forwards and chapter roundups	[ ]	[ ]	[ ]
Quick quizzes	[ ]	[ ]	[ ]
Question Bank	[ ]	[ ]	[ ]
Answer Bank	[ ]	[ ]	[ ]
Index	[ ]	[ ]	[ ]
Icons	[ ]	[ ]	[ ]

	Excellent	Good	Adequate	Poor
Overall opinion of this Study Text	[ ]	[ ]	[ ]	[ ]

Do you intend to continue using BPP products? [ ] Yes [ ] No

On the reverse of this page are noted particular areas of the text about which we would welcome your feedback.

The BPP author of this edition can be e-mailed at: lmfeedback@bpp.com

Please return this form to: BPP Publishing Services, Aldine Place, 142-144 Uxbridge Road, London, W12 8AA

Review Form (continued)

TELL US WHAT YOU THINK

Please note any further comments and suggestions/errors below